# The Great American BANJO SONGBOOK

Banjo Arrangements by Alan Munde and Beth Mead-Sullivan

ISBN 978-1-4950-5976-6

Visit Hal Leonard Online at www.halleonard.com

HAL•LEONARD®
7777 WEST BLUEMOUND ROAD MILWAUKEE, WI 53213

# CONTENTS

*C tuning

# PREFACE

**B**luegrass-style banjo players have been arranging melodies from the Great American Songbook since the earliest days of bluegrass music. In a seminal recording session of the Flatt and Scruggs ensemble, Earl Scruggs waxed the now oft-played "Farewell Blues." Another early stylist, Don Reno, with an eye to expanding the audience for bluegrass-type banjo playing, recorded many Songbook standards. His repertoire included "Beer Barrel Polka," "Limehouse Blues," "The World Is Waiting for the Sunrise," "Birth of the Blues," and others. Well-known players followed their lead, with Allen Shelton popularizing his arrangement of "Lady of Spain." Eddie Adcock, Roger Sprung, and Bill Keith were notable in their adaptations of the works of the best of American popular song composers for the three-fingered bluegrass banjo style.

We offer this book with the hope that our fellow bluegrass banjo players will find appealing songs and arrangements here to enhance and enrich their repertoire, with the goal of broadening the audience appeal of the bluegrass banjo. Though carefully crafted, we present these not as the final word, but as a beginning point for further exploration.

Alan Munde
Beth Mead-Sullivan

# The Glow Worm

**Modern Version by Johnny Mercer**
**Original Lyric by Lilla Cayley Robinson**
**Music by Paul Lincke**

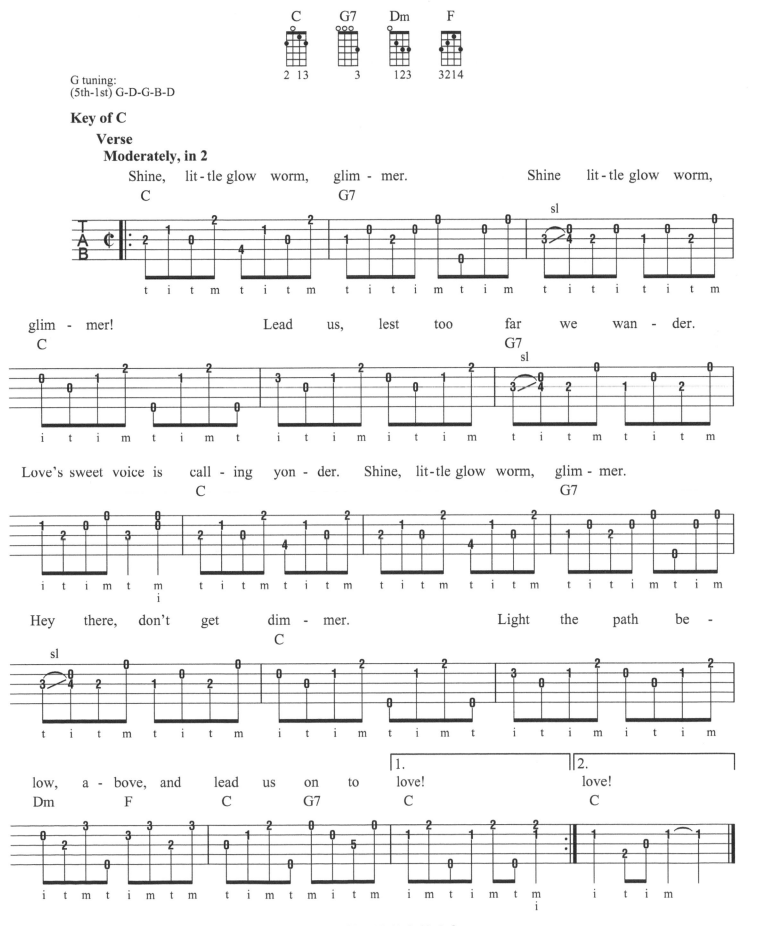

# After You've Gone

from ONE MO' TIME
Words by Henry Creamer
Music by Turner Layton

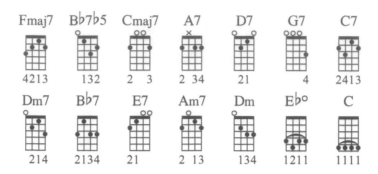

G tuning:
(5th-1st) G-D-G-B-D

**Key of C**

**Verse**

**Bright**

Af - ter you've gone and left me cry - ing,

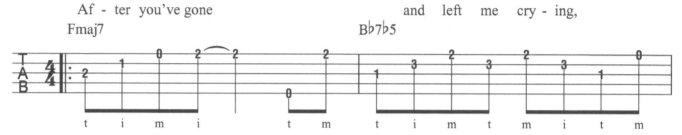

af - ter you've gone, there's no de - ny - ing

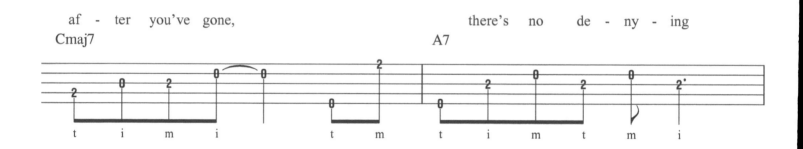

you'll feel blue, you'll feel sad.

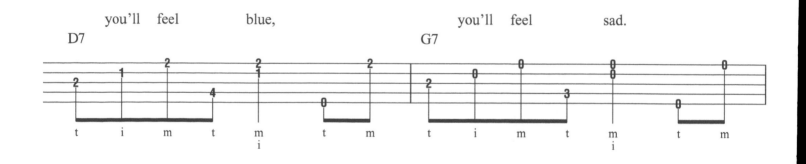

You'll miss the dear - est pal you've ev - er had.

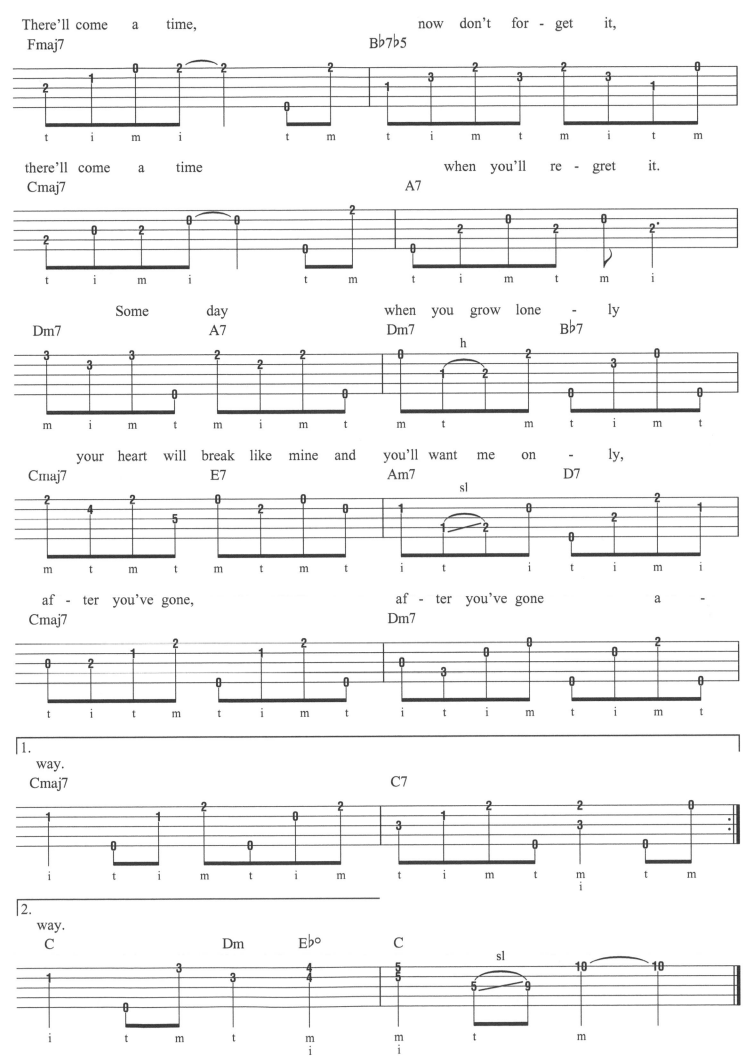

# Ain't She Sweet

Words by Jack Yellen
Music by Milton Ager

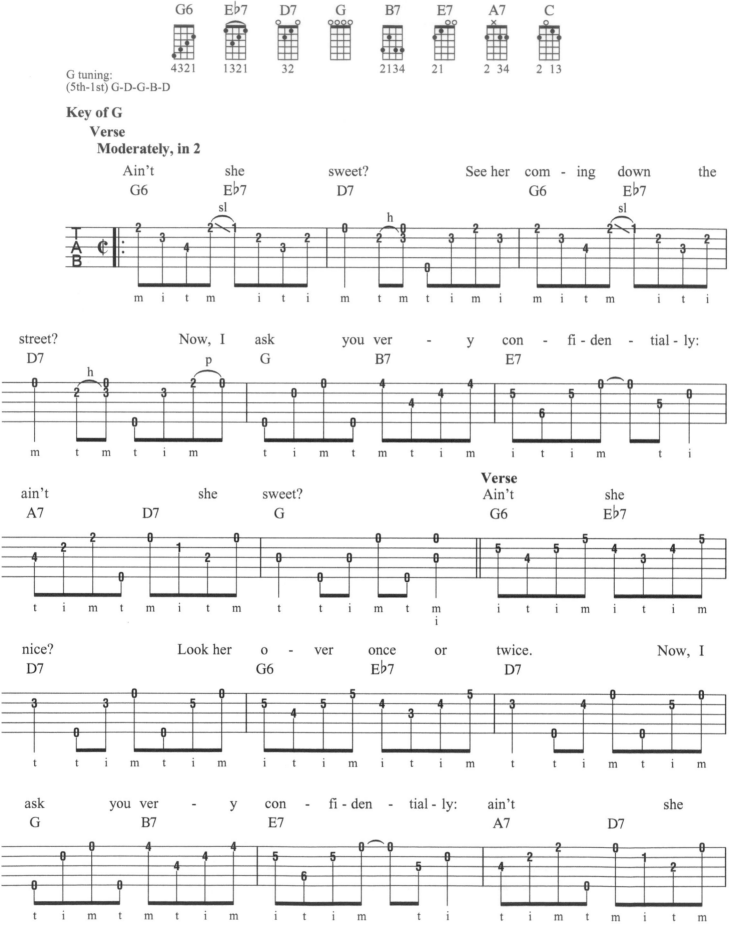

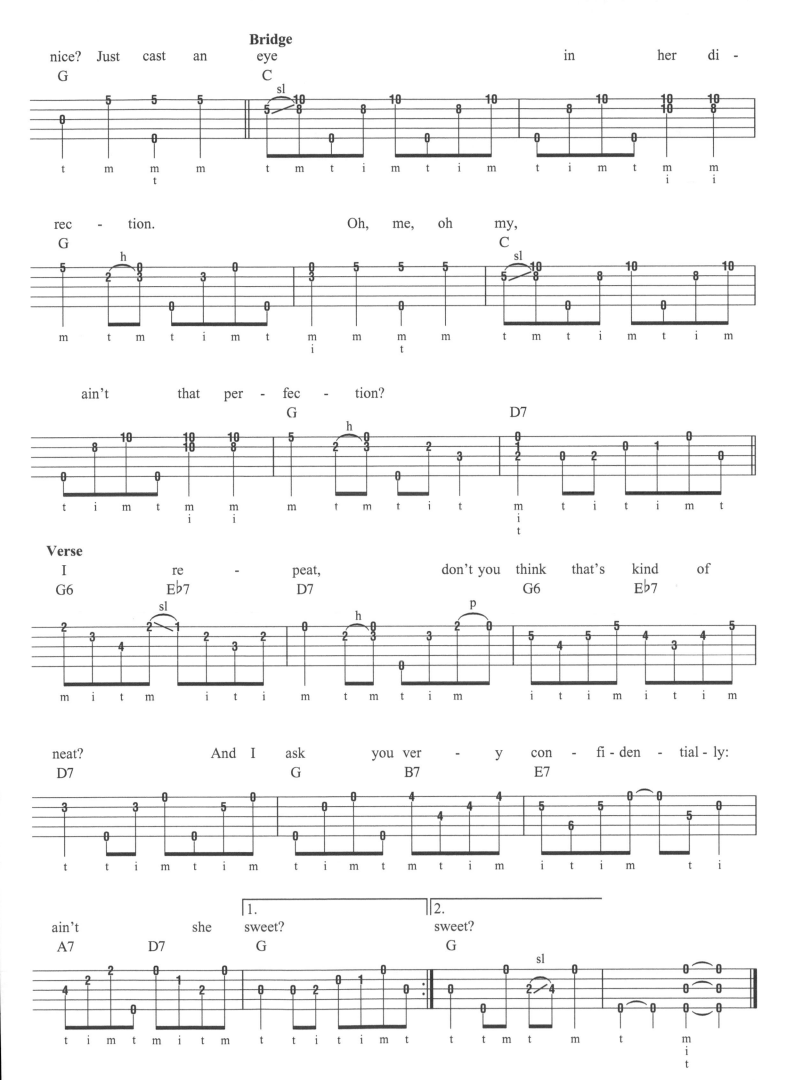

# All of Me

**Words and Music by Seymour Simons and Gerald Marks**

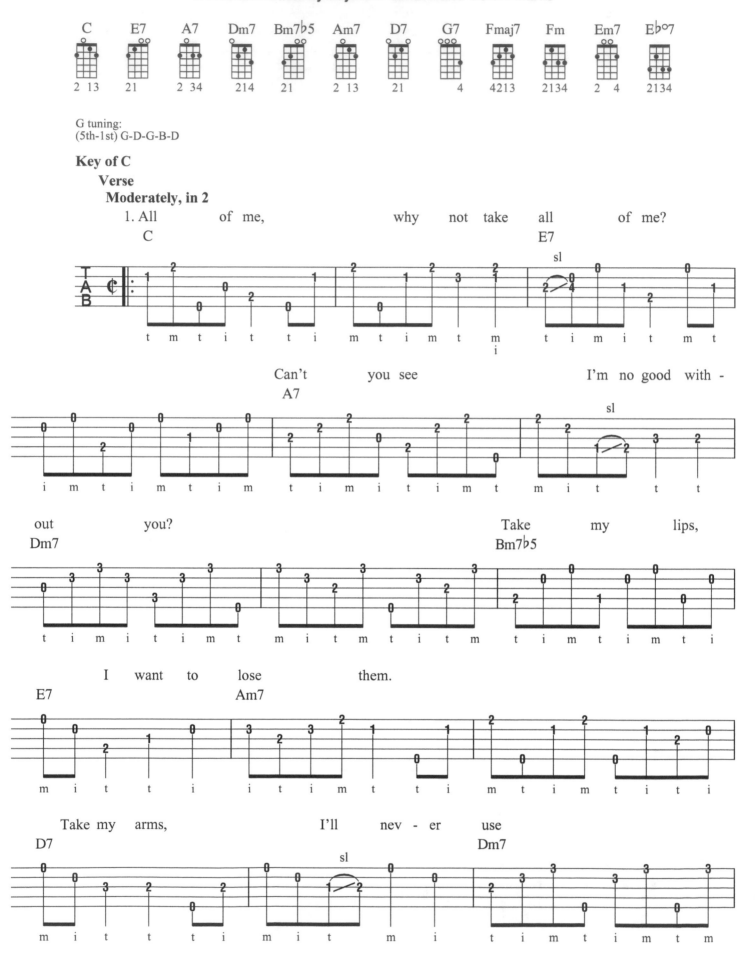

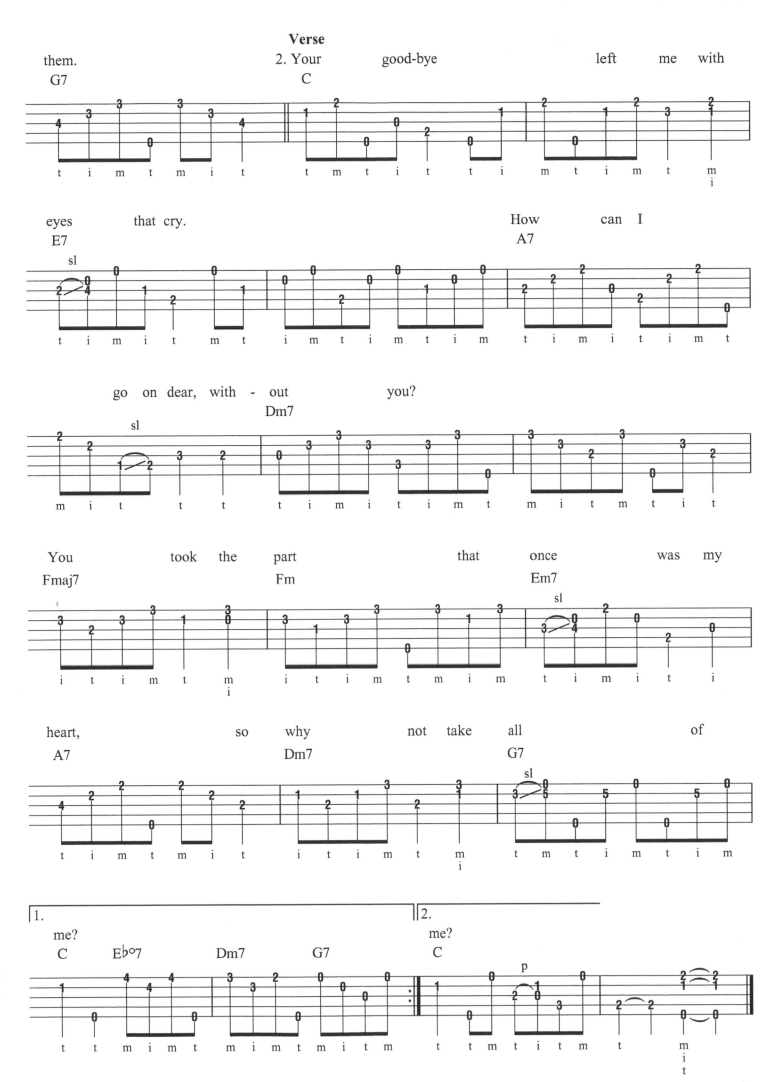

# All the Things You Are

**from VERY WARM FOR MAY**
Lyrics by Oscar Hammerstein II
Music by Jerome Kern

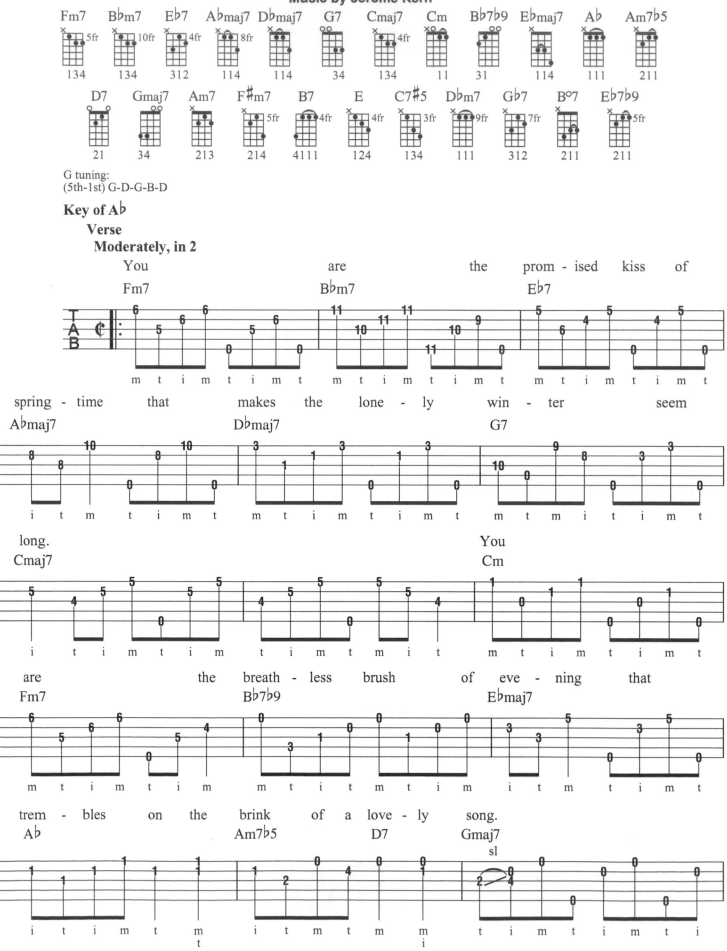

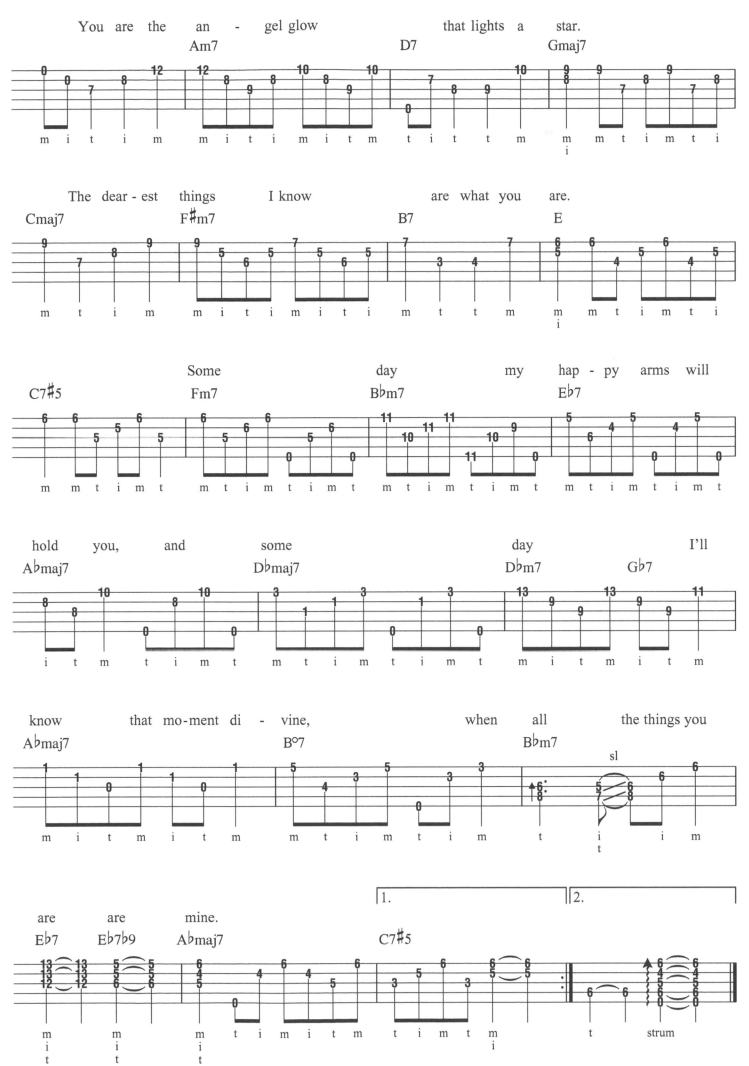

# Always

**Words and Music by Irving Berlin**

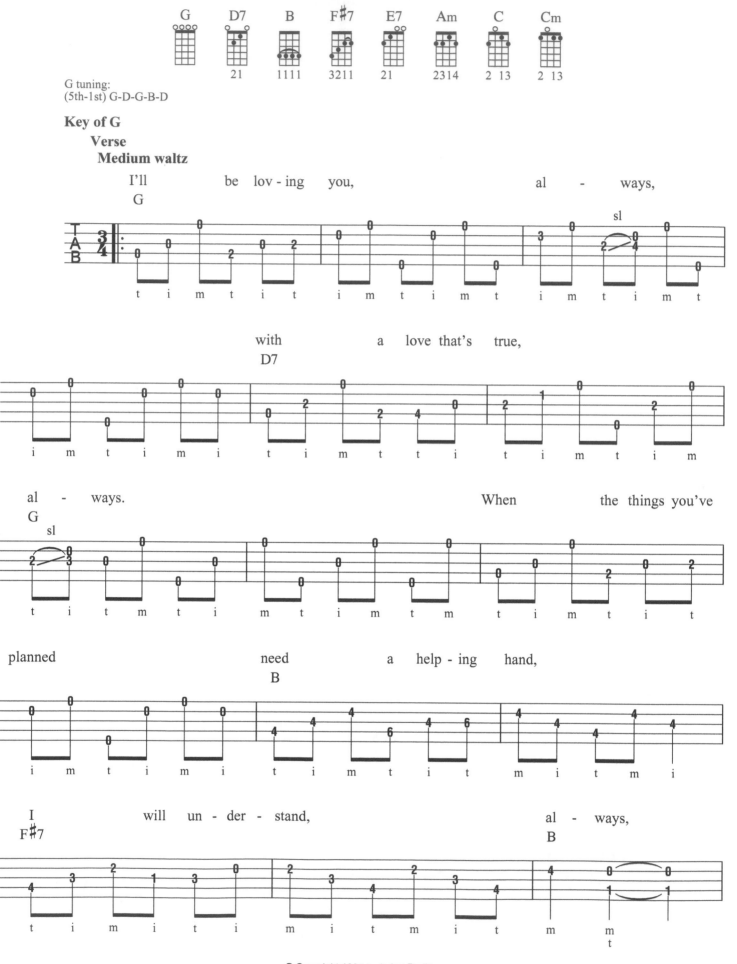

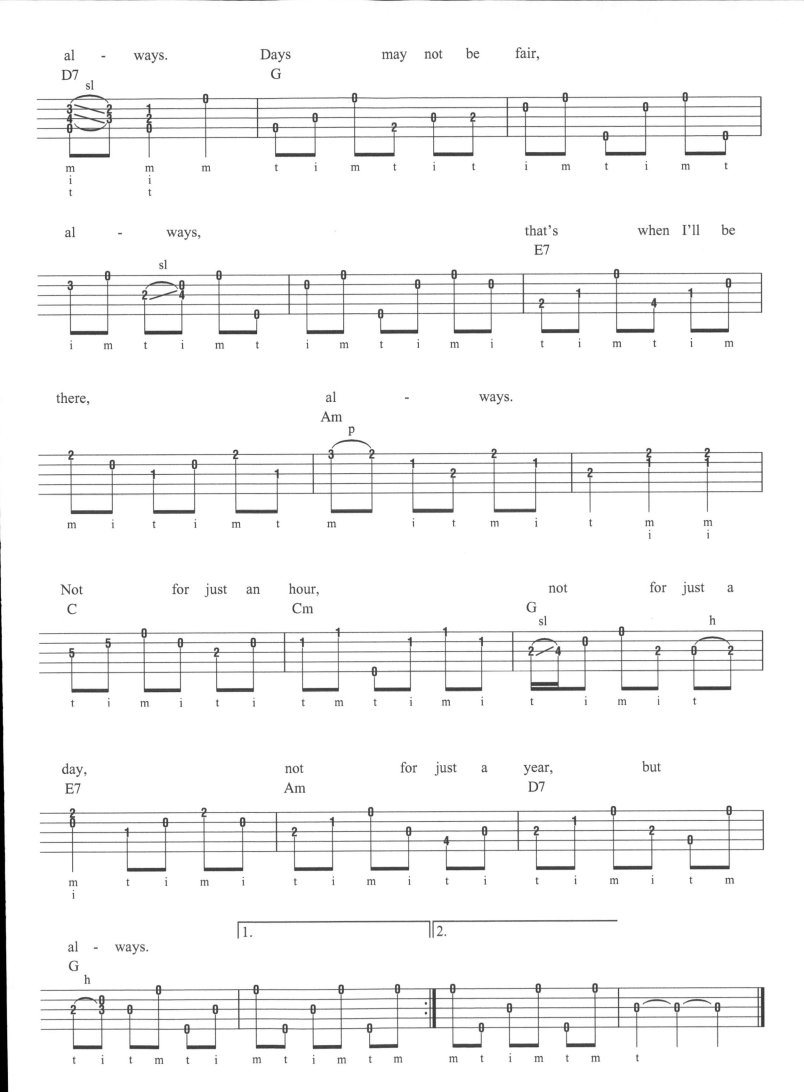

# Anchors Aweigh

**Words by Alfred Hart Miles and Royal Lovell**
**Music by Charles A. Zimmerman**
**Additional Lyric by George D. Lottman**

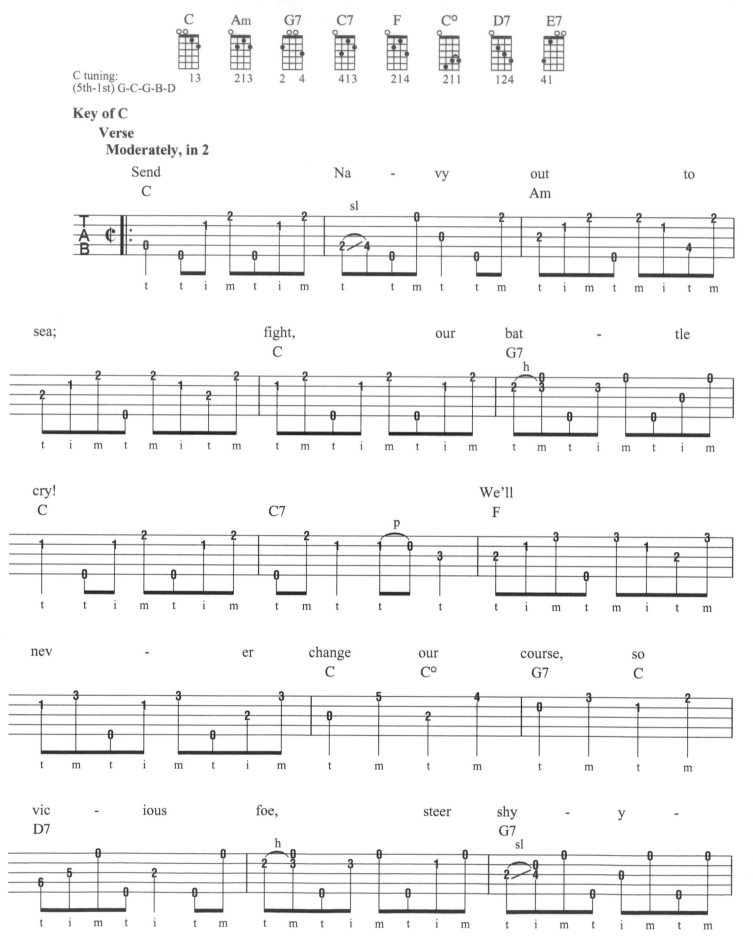

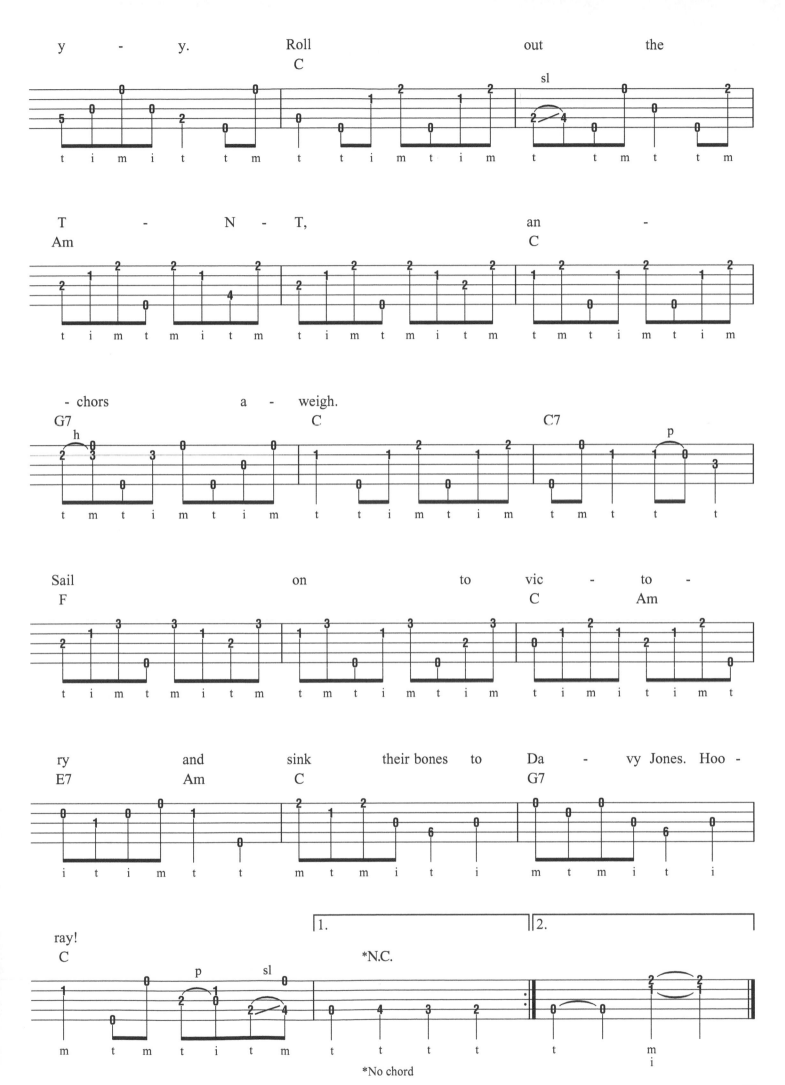

# Avalon

**Words by Al Jolson and B.G. DeSylva**
**Music by Vincent Rose**

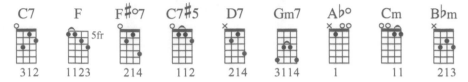

C tuning:
(5th-1st) G-C-G-B-D

**Key of F**

**Verse**

**Moderately, in 2**

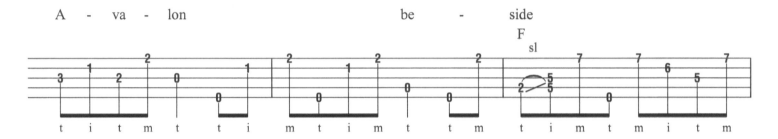

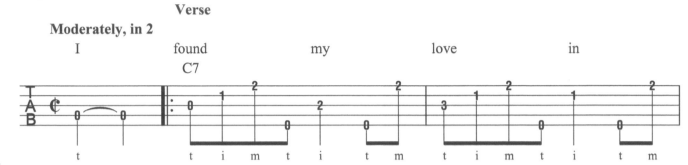

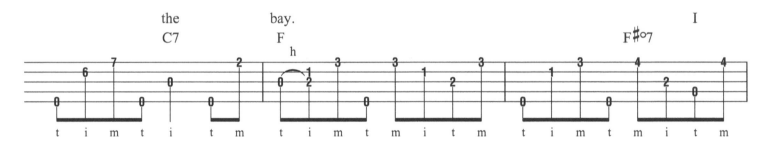

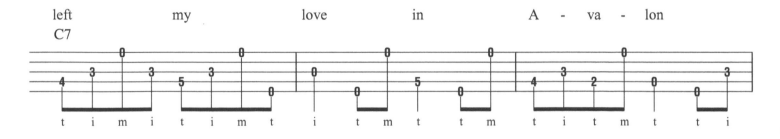

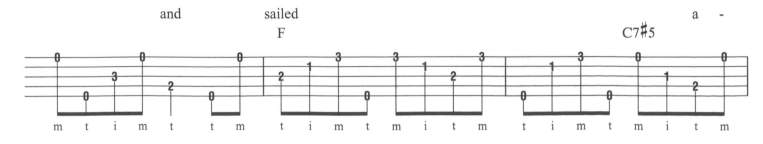

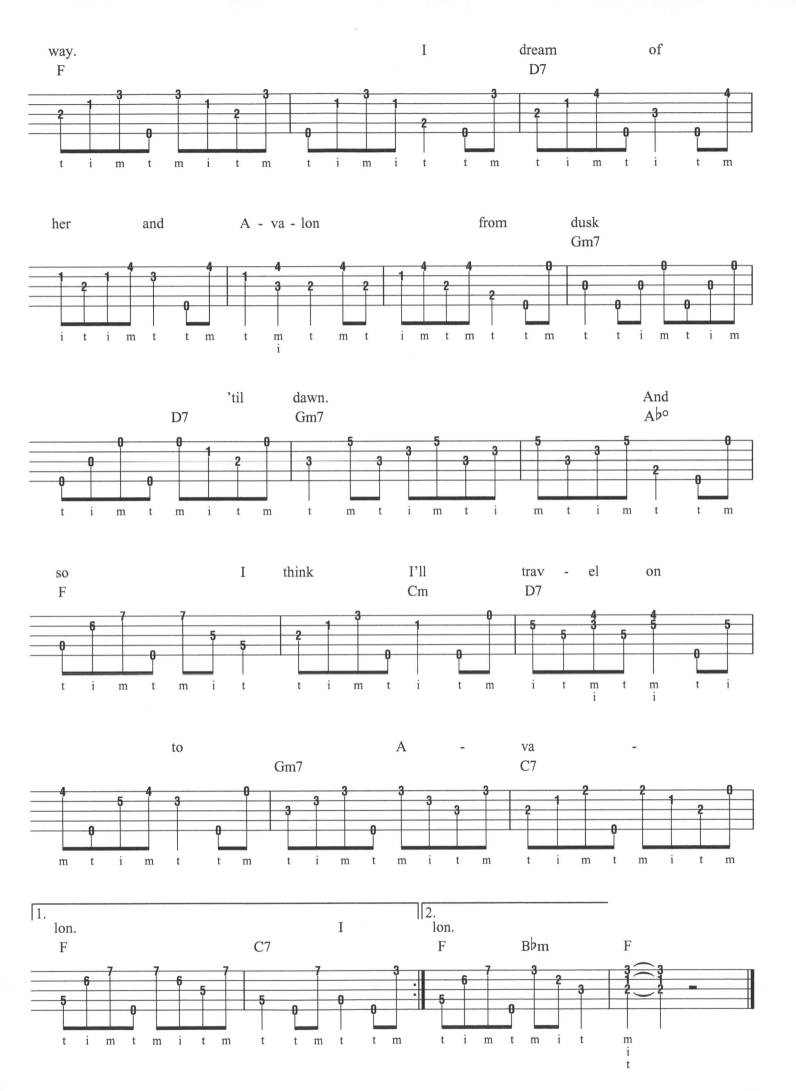

# Baby Face

**Words and Music by Benny Davis and Harry Akst**

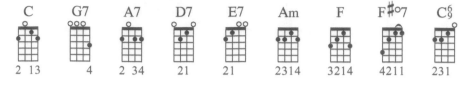

G tuning:
(5th-1st) G-D-G-B-D

**Key of C**
    **Verse**
      **Moderately, in 2**

Ba - by Face, you've got the

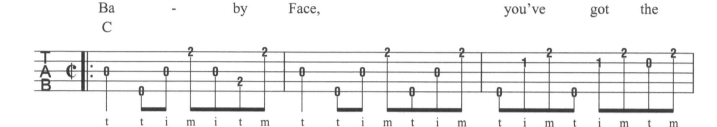

cut - est lit - tle ba - by face.

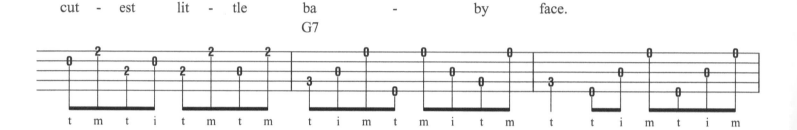

There's not a - noth - er one to take your

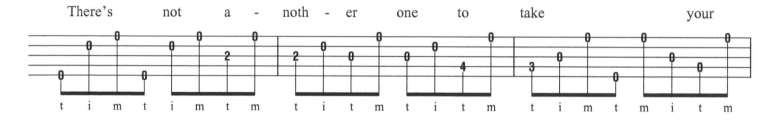

place, Ba - by Face.

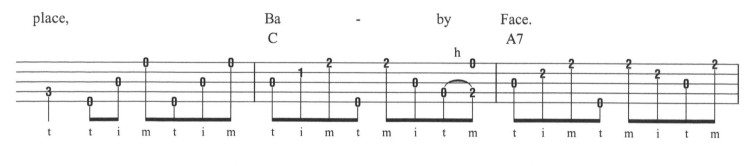

My poor heart is jump - in'. You sure have start -

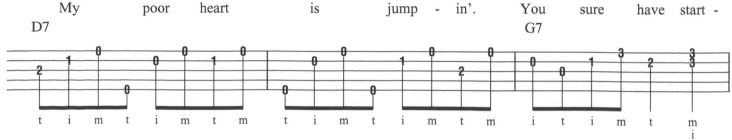

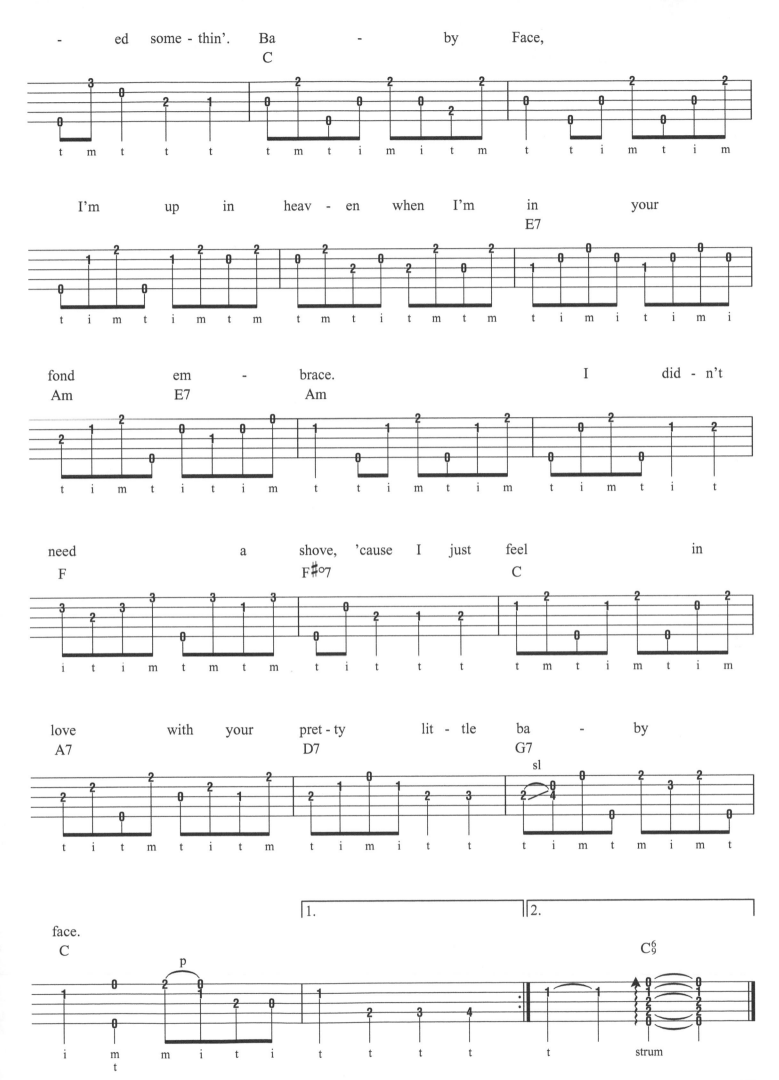

# Back in the Saddle Again

**Words and Music by Gene Autry and Ray Whitley**

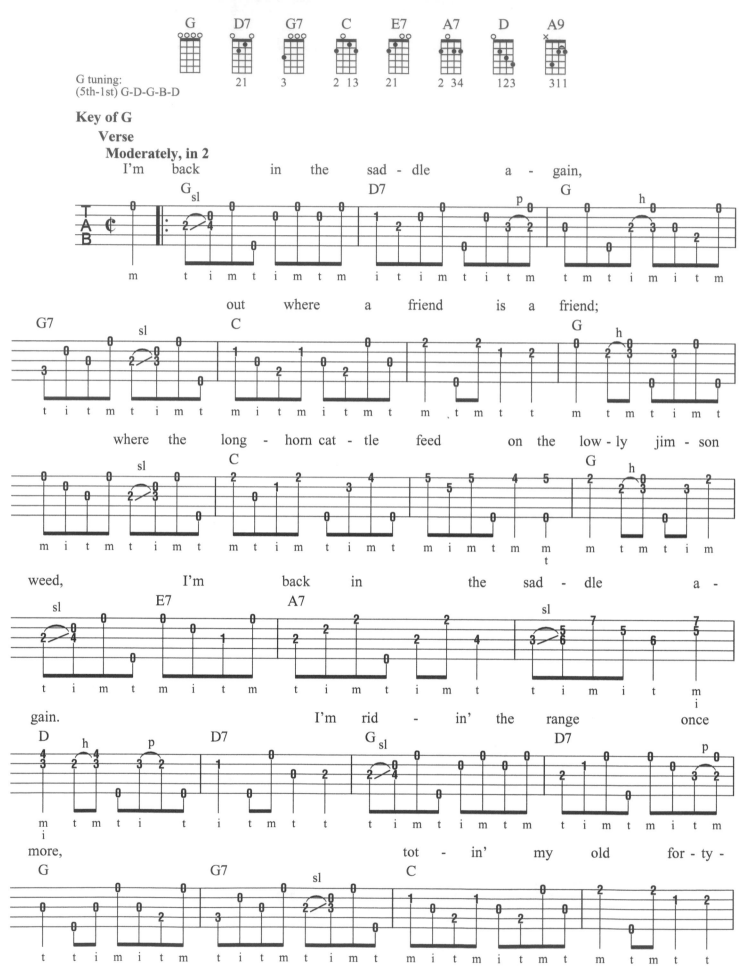

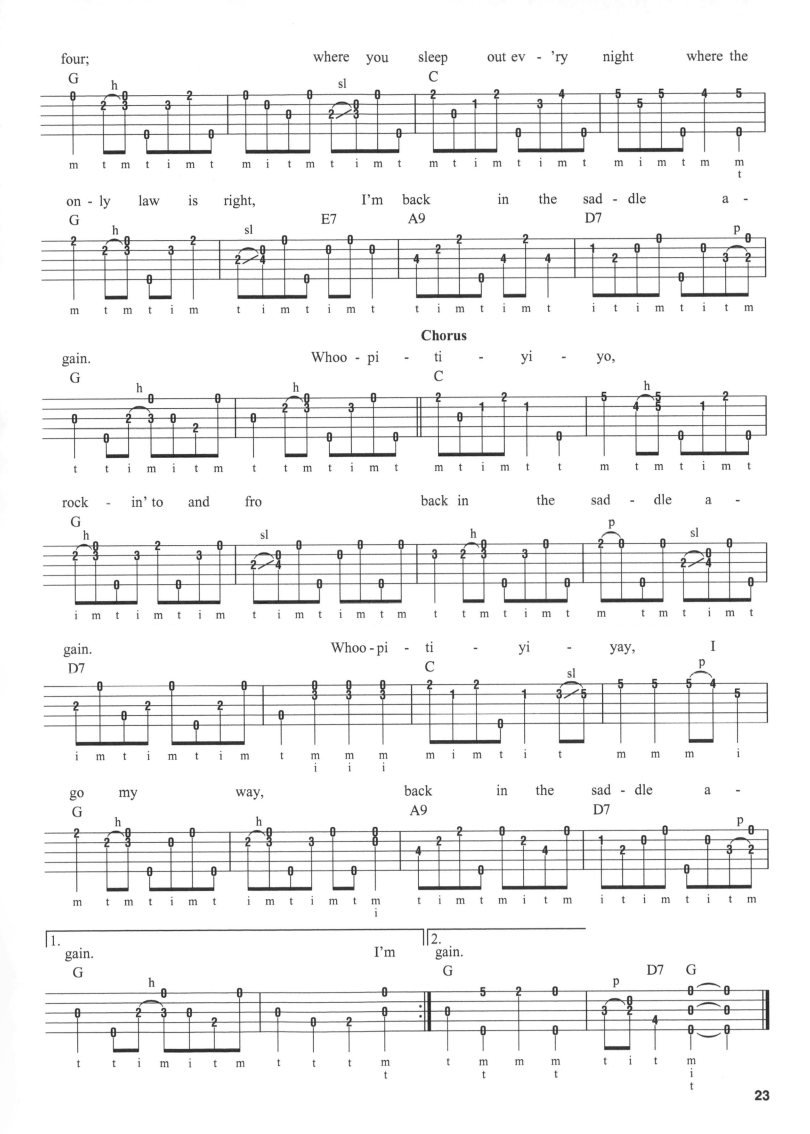

# The Bells of St. Mary's

**Words by Douglas Furber**
**Music by A. Emmett Adams**

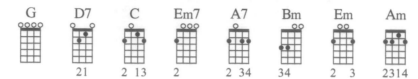

G tuning:
(5th-1st) G-D-G-B-D

**Key of G**
   **Verse**
     **Moderately, in 2**

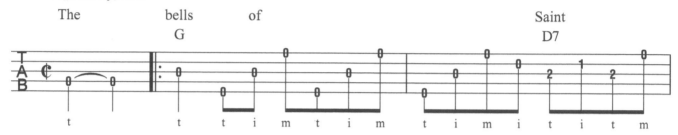

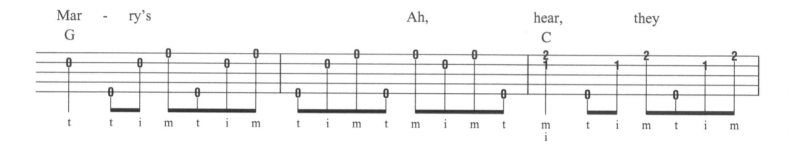

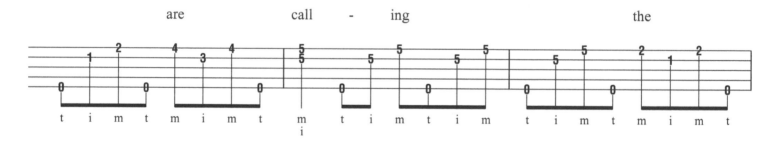

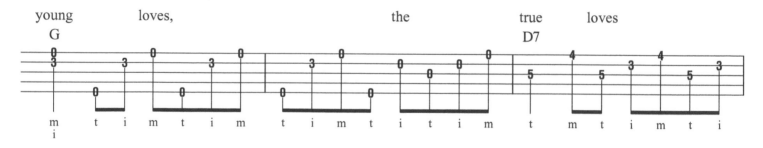

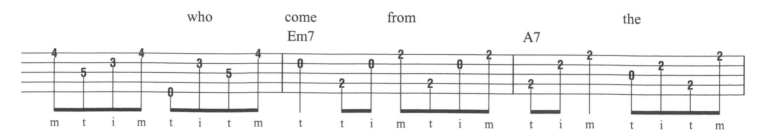

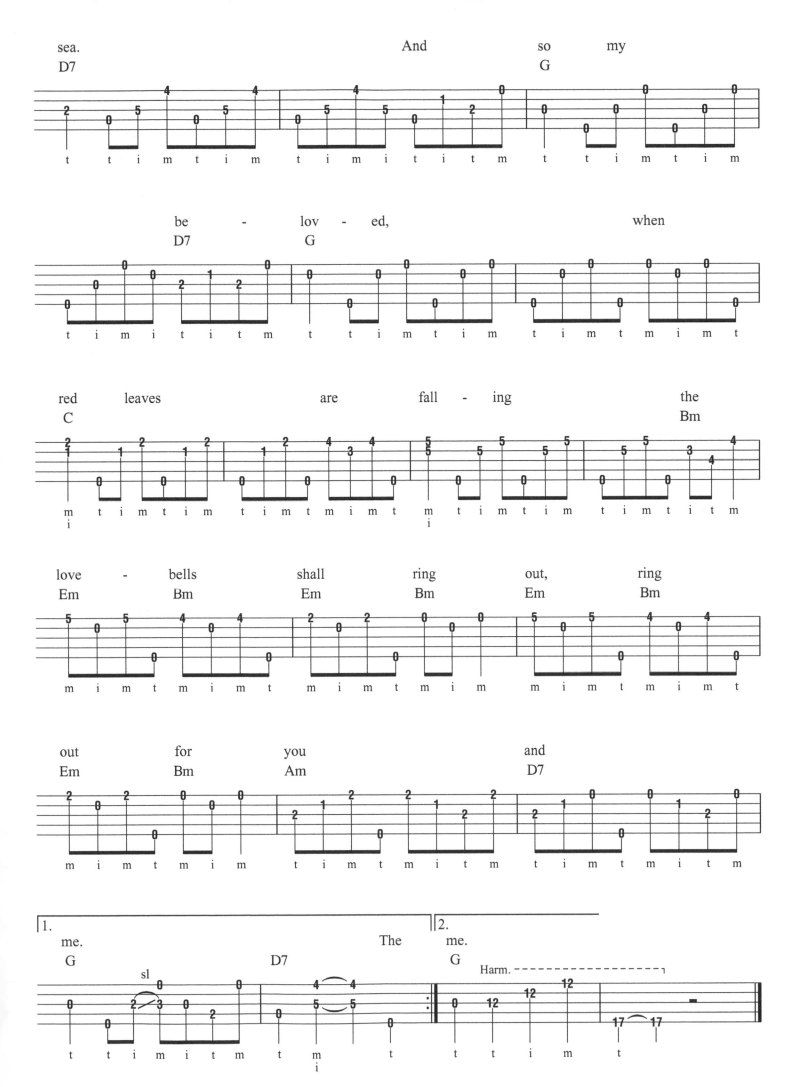

# Blue Skies

## from BETSY
### Words and Music by Irving Berlin

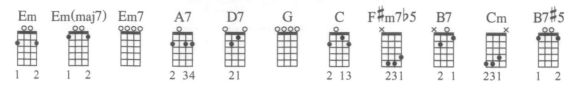

G tuning:
(5th-1st) G-D-G-B-D

**Key of G**

𝄋 **Verse**
**Moderately**

1. Blue      skies      smil - ing    at
2. Blue      birds      sing - ing    a

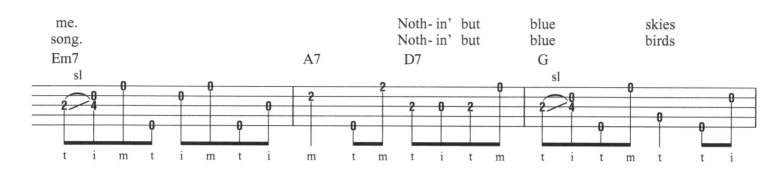

me.
song.

     Noth- in' but    blue      skies
     Noth- in' but    blue      birds

do   I      |1. see.
from   now

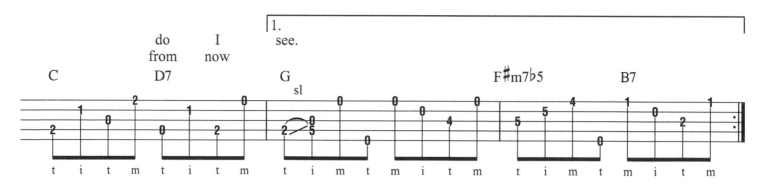

|2.

on.

**Bridge**
Nev - er   saw   the   sun

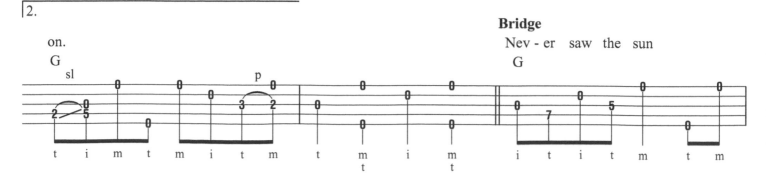

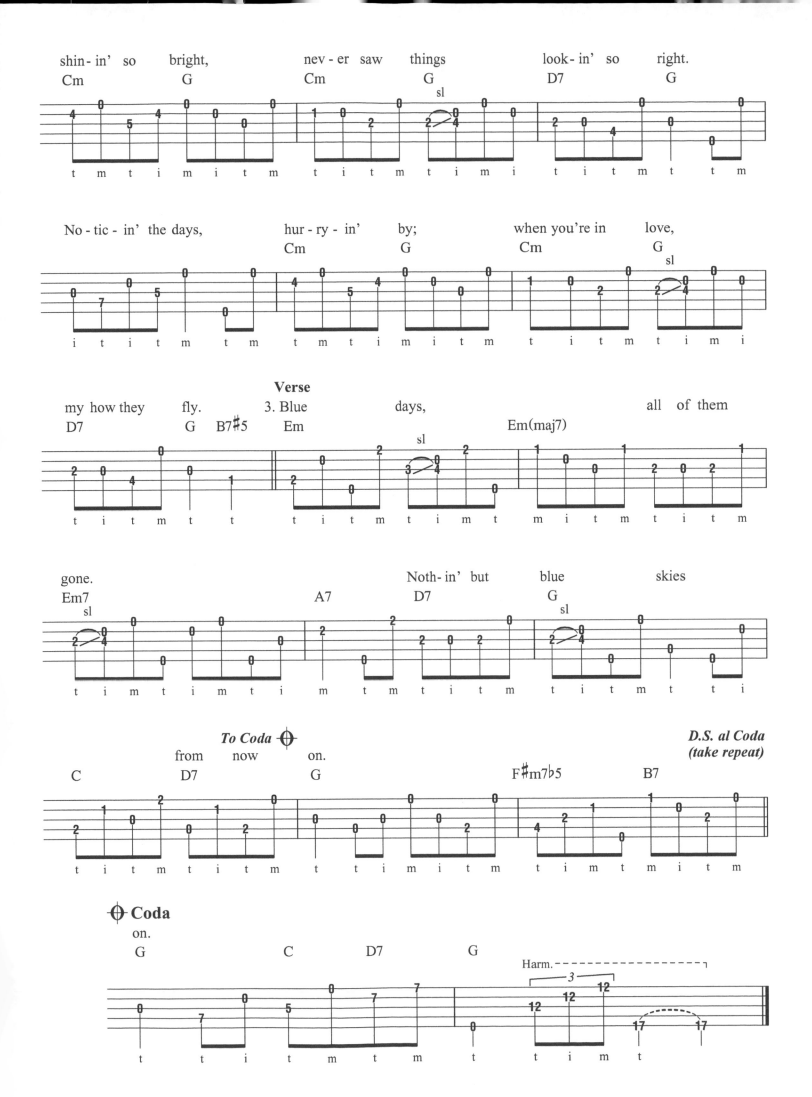

# But Not for Me

## from GIRL CRAZY

### Music and Lyrics by George Gershwin and Ira Gershwin

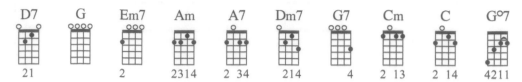

G tuning:
(5th-1st) G-D-G-B-D

**Key of G**

**Verse**

**Moderately, in 2**

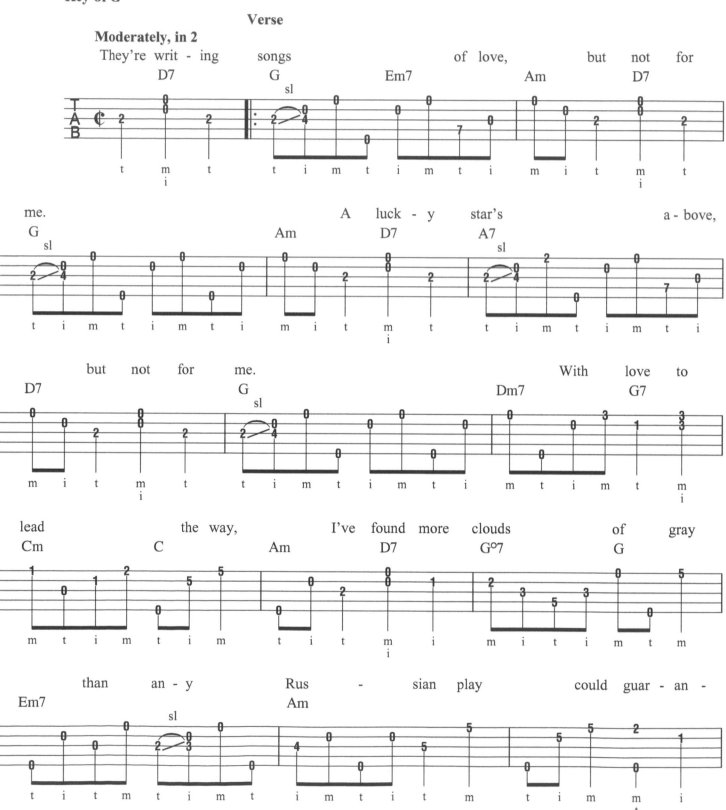

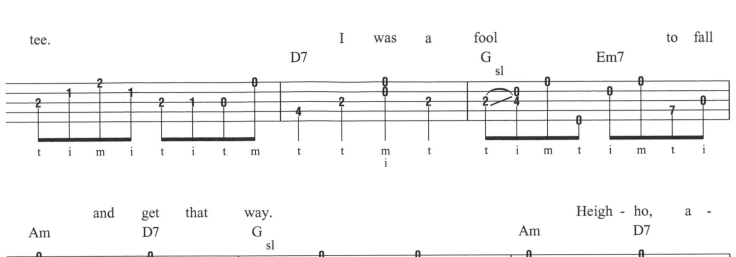

tee.         I    was    a    fool            to  fall

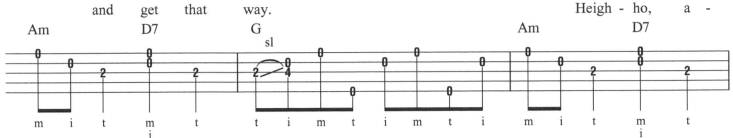

and  get  that  way.          Heigh - ho,  a -

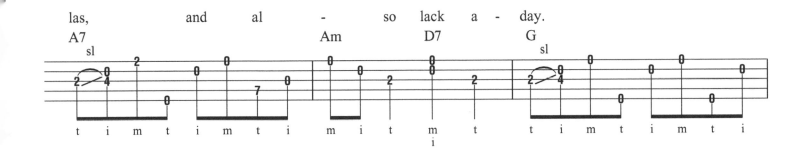

las,     and  al - so  lack a - day.

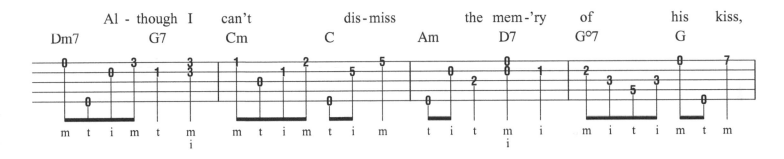

Al - though I  can't    dis - miss   the mem-'ry  of   his  kiss,

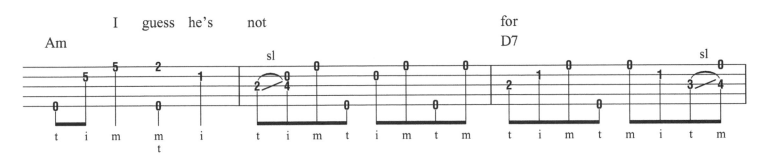

I  guess he's  not         for

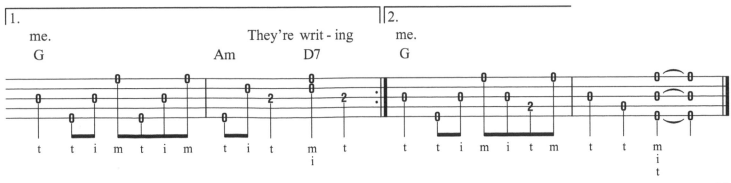

1.    me.       They're writ - ing   2.  me.

# California, Here I Come

### Words and Music by Al Jolson, B.G. DeSylva and Joseph Meyer

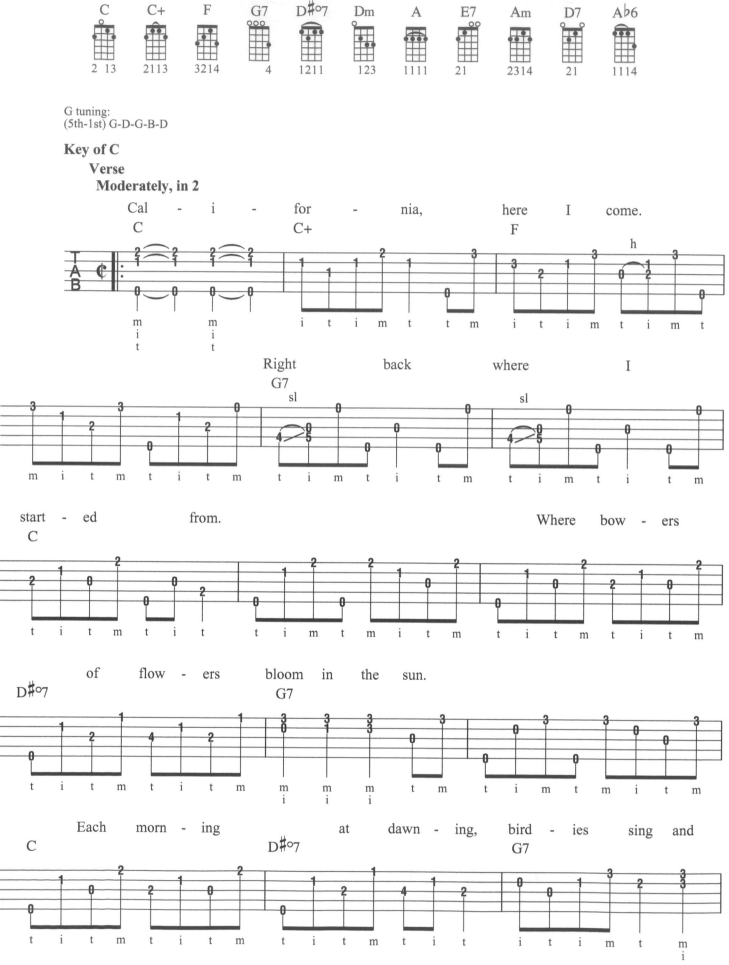

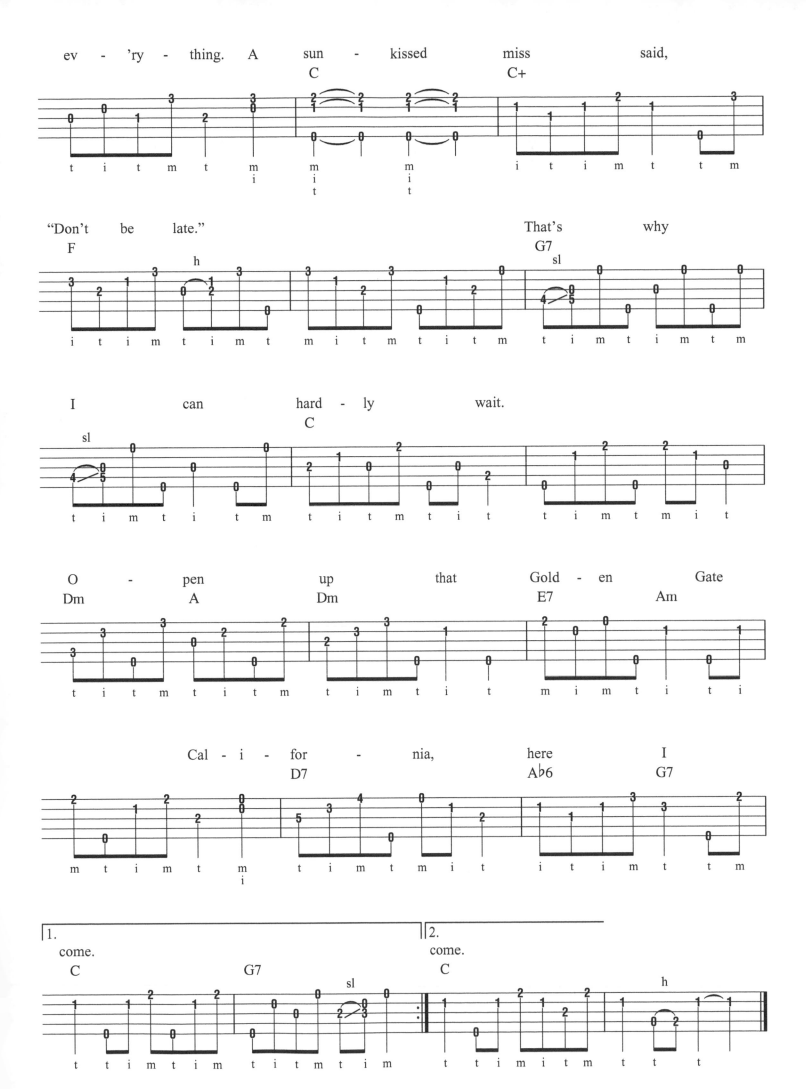

# Charmaine

**Words and Music by Lew Pollack and Erno Rapee**

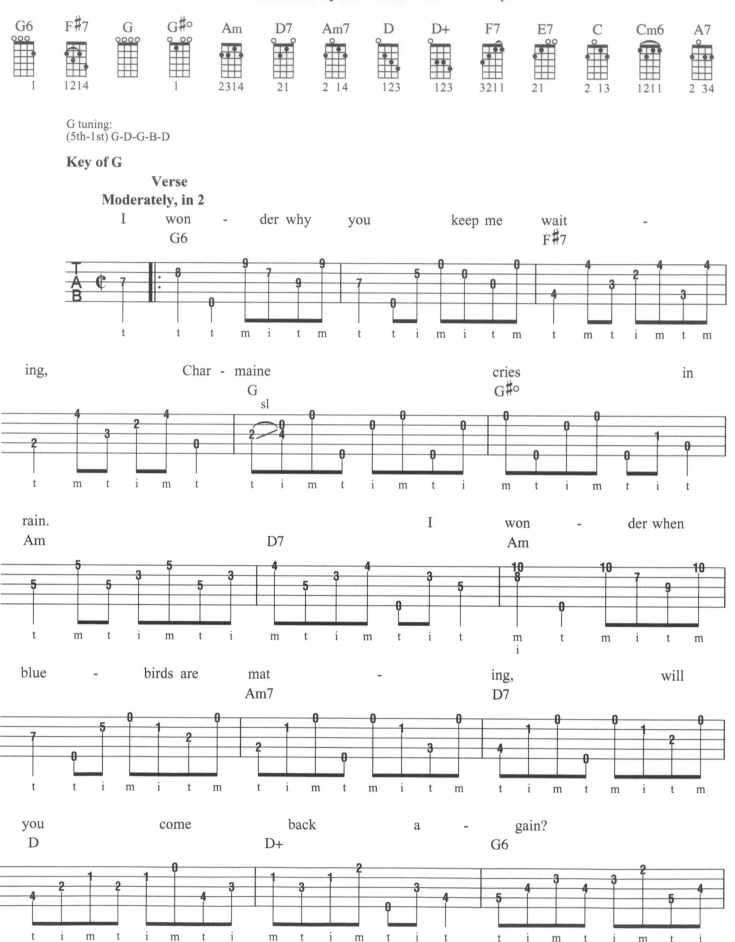

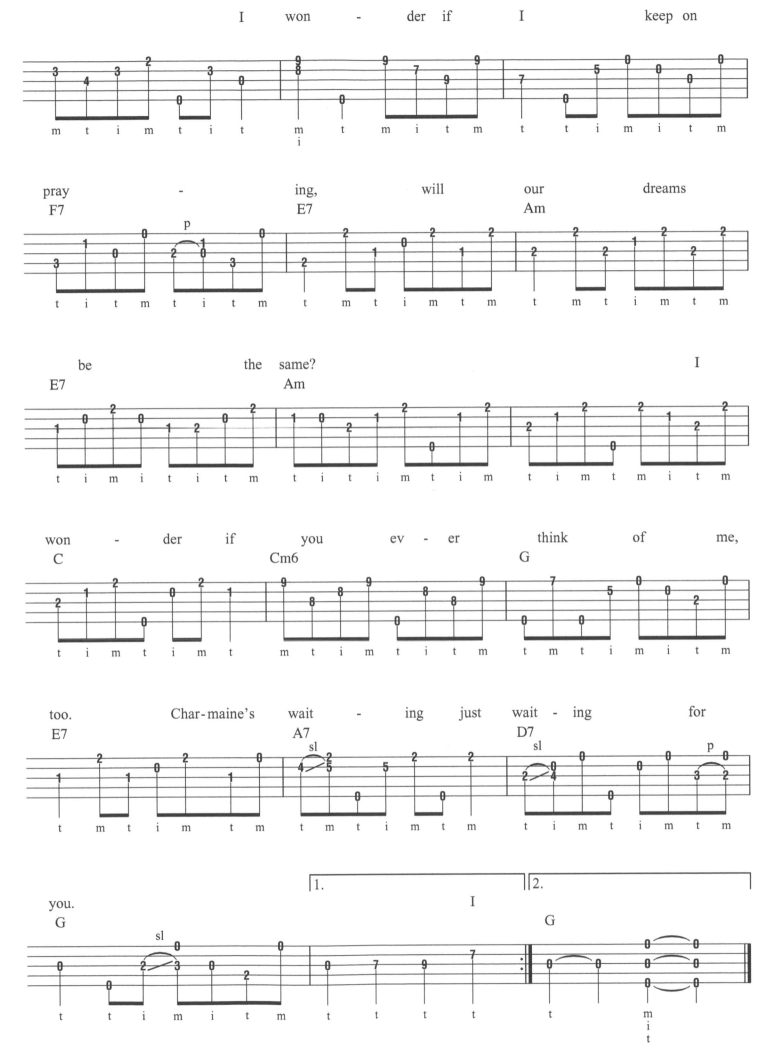

# Cheek to Cheek

from the RKO Radio Motion Picture TOP HAT
Words and Music by Irving Berlin

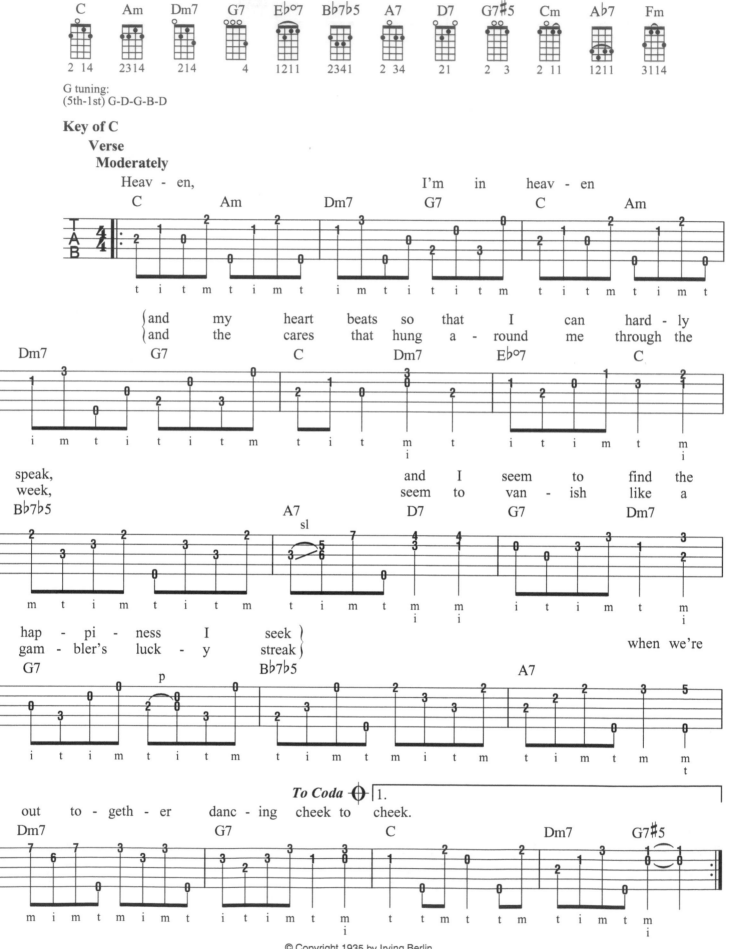

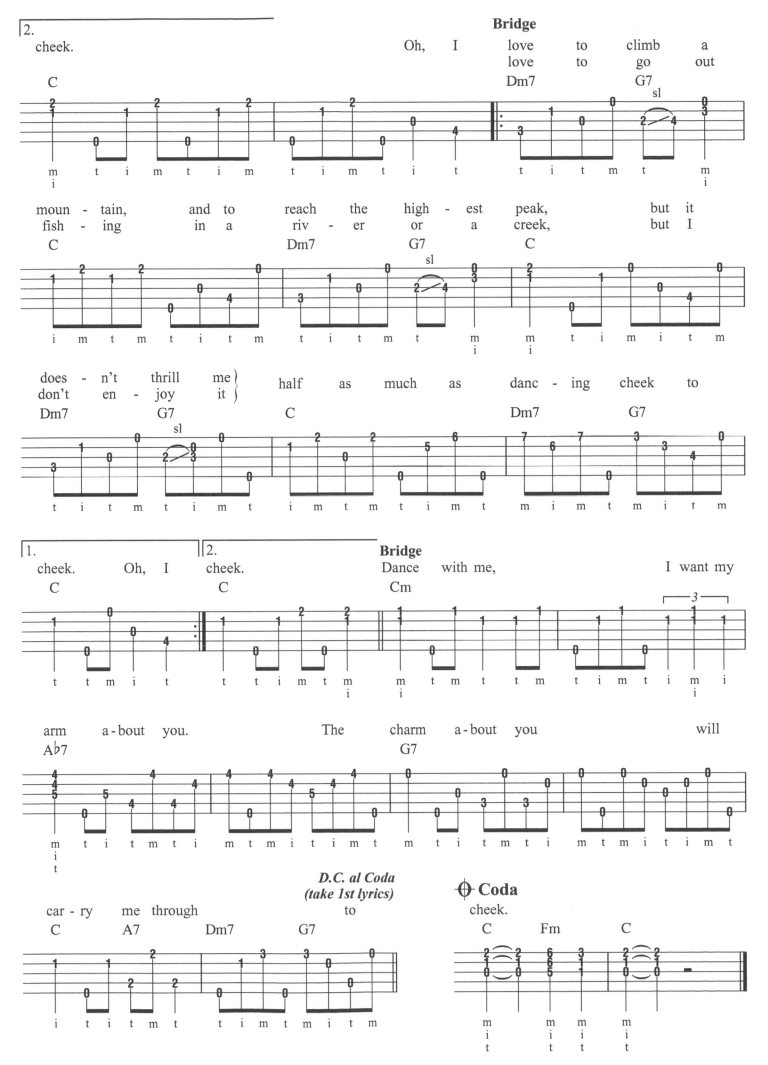

# Don't Sit Under the Apple Tree
## (With Anyone Else but Me)

**Words and Music by Lew Brown, Sam H. Stept and Charlie Tobias**

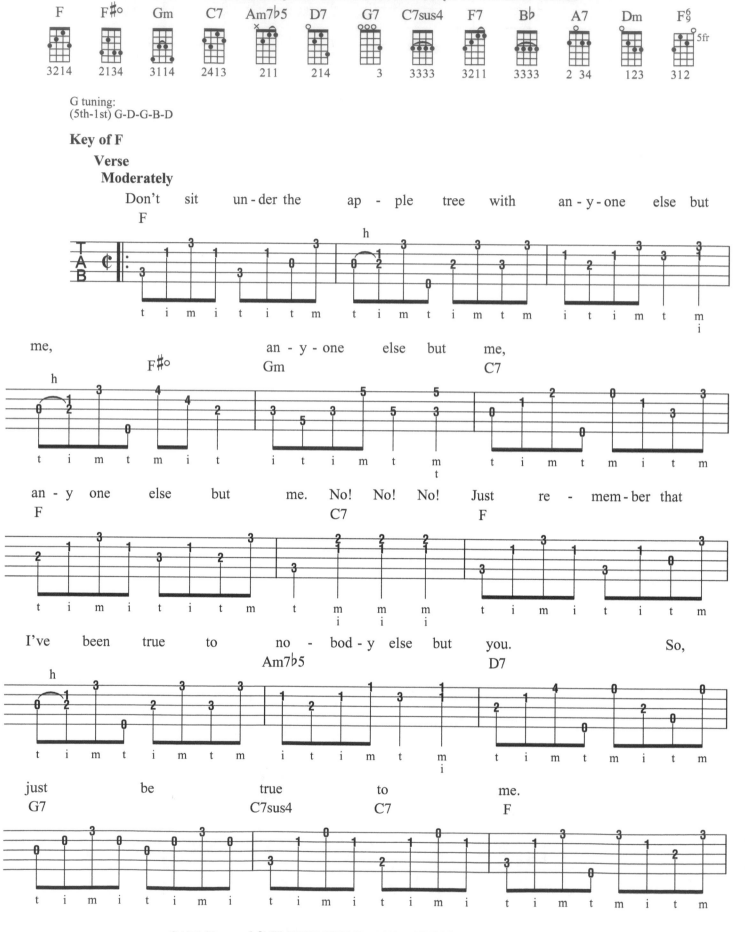

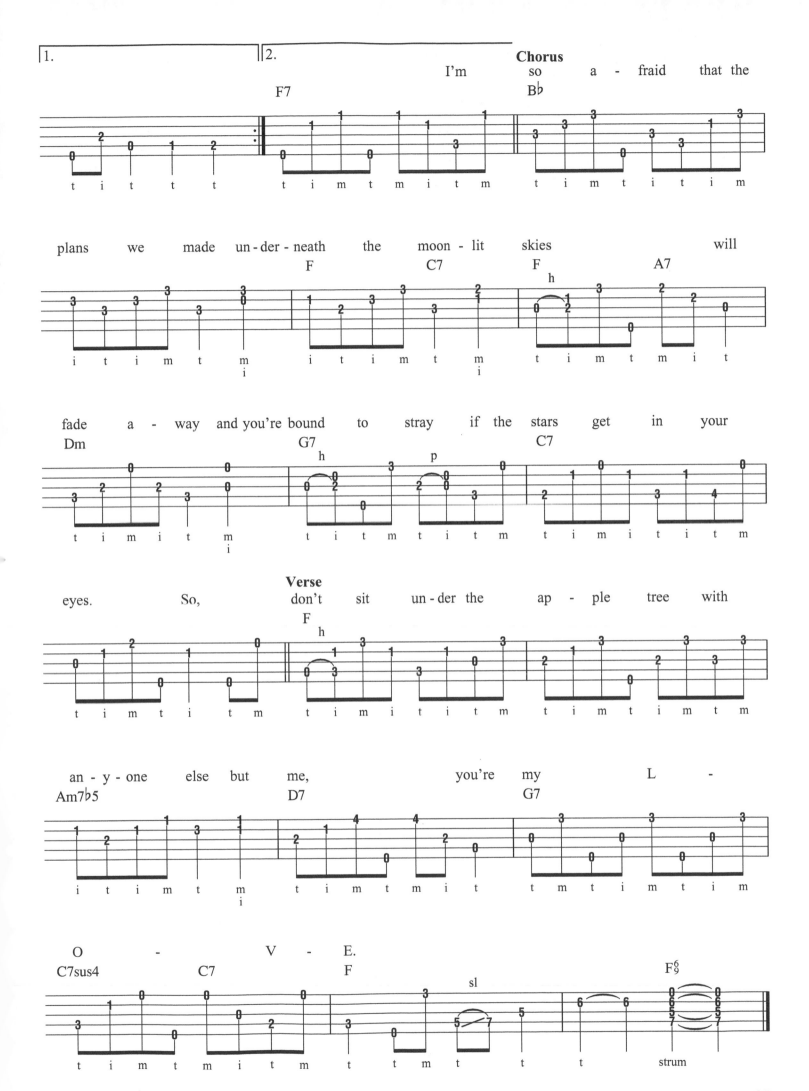

# Dream a Little Dream of Me

**Words by Gus Kahn**
**Music by Wilbur Schwandt and Fabian Andree**

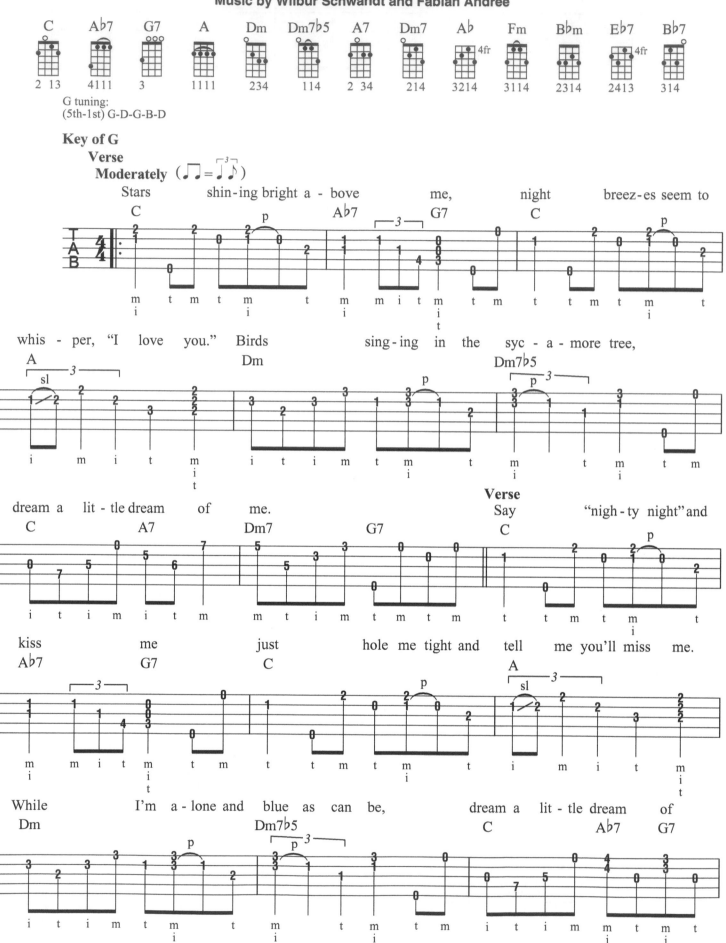

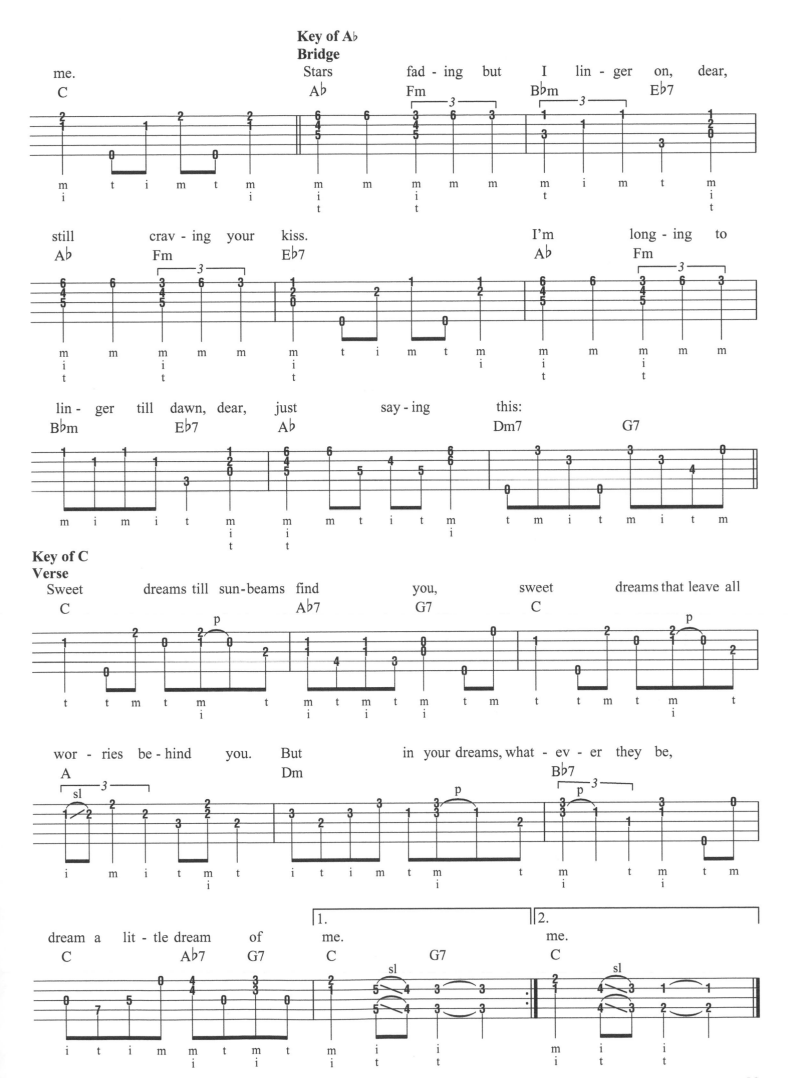

# Elmer's Tune

Words and Music by Elmer Albrecht, Sammy Gallop and Dick Jurgens

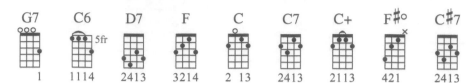

G tuning:
(5th-1st) G-D-G-B-D

**Key of C**

**Verse**

**Moderately**

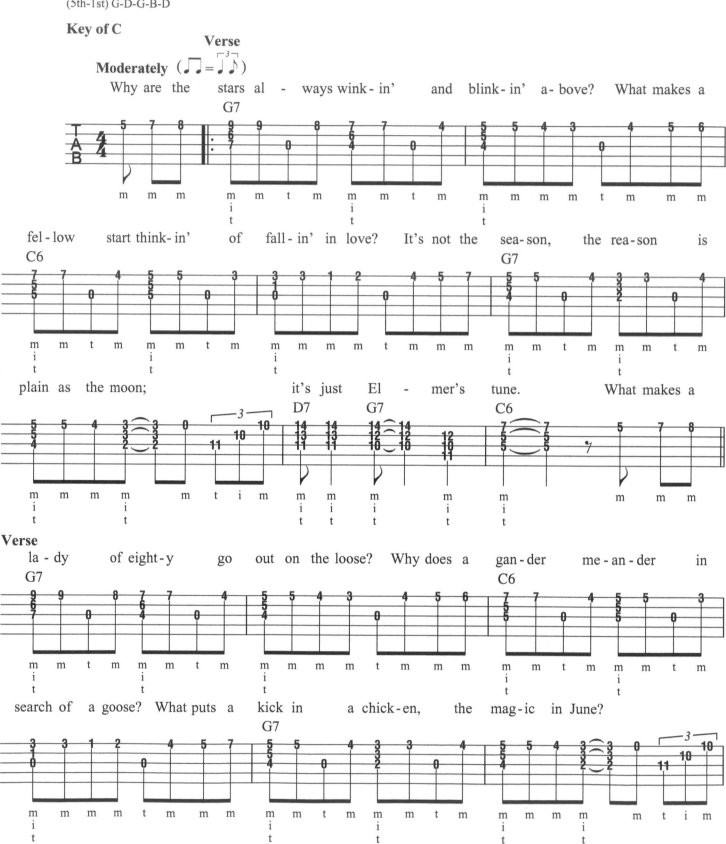

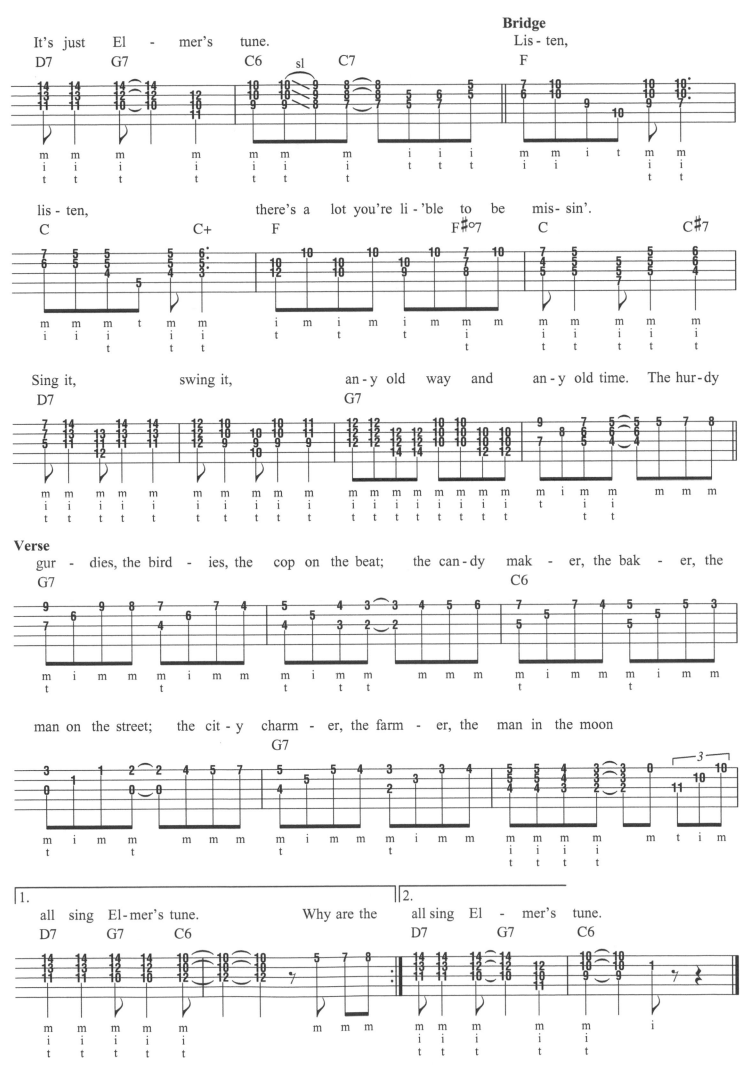

# Embraceable You

### from CRAZY FOR YOU
### Music and Lyrics by George Gershwin and Ira Gershwin

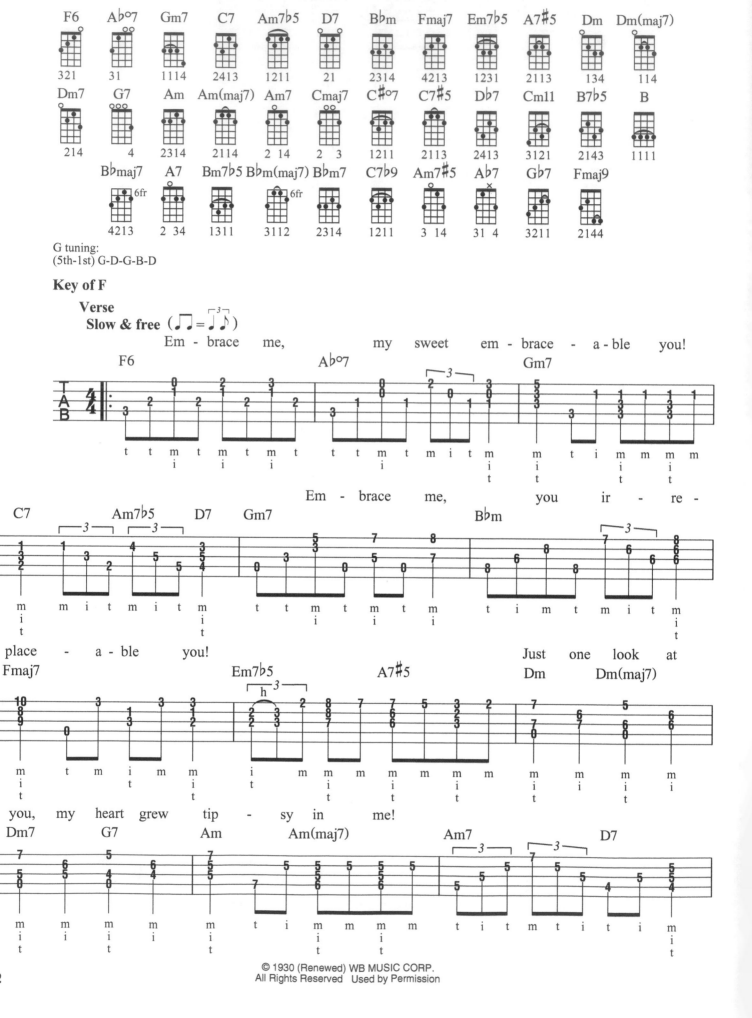

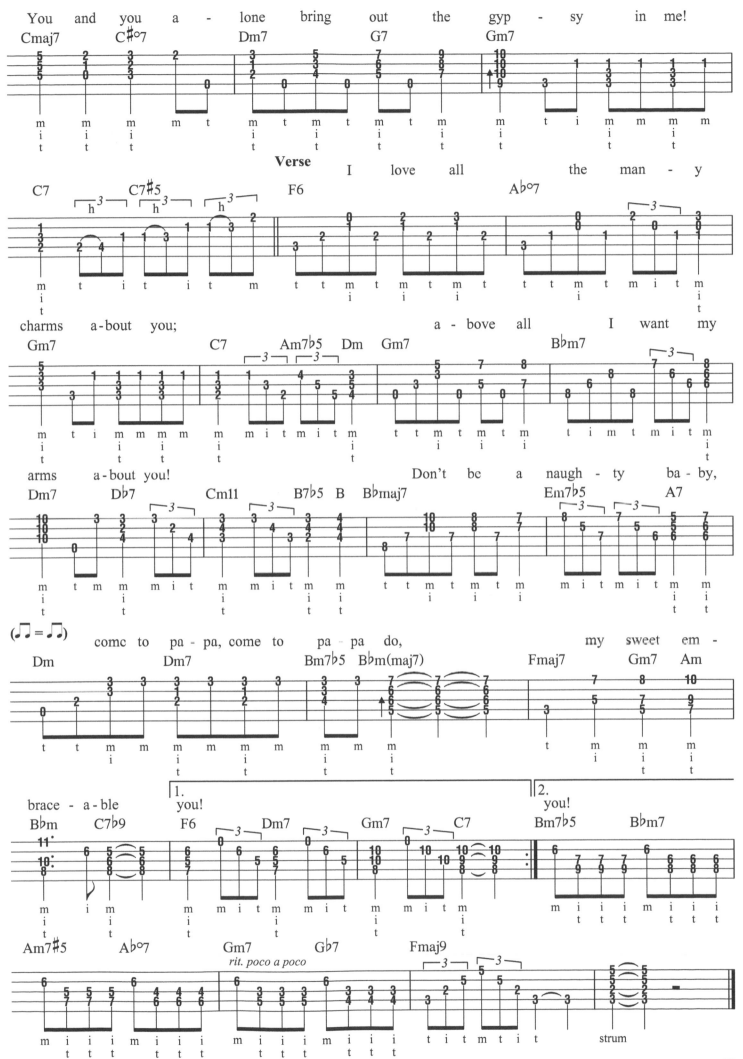

# A Fine Romance

## from SWING TIME

**Words by Dorothy Fields**
**Music by Jerome Kern**

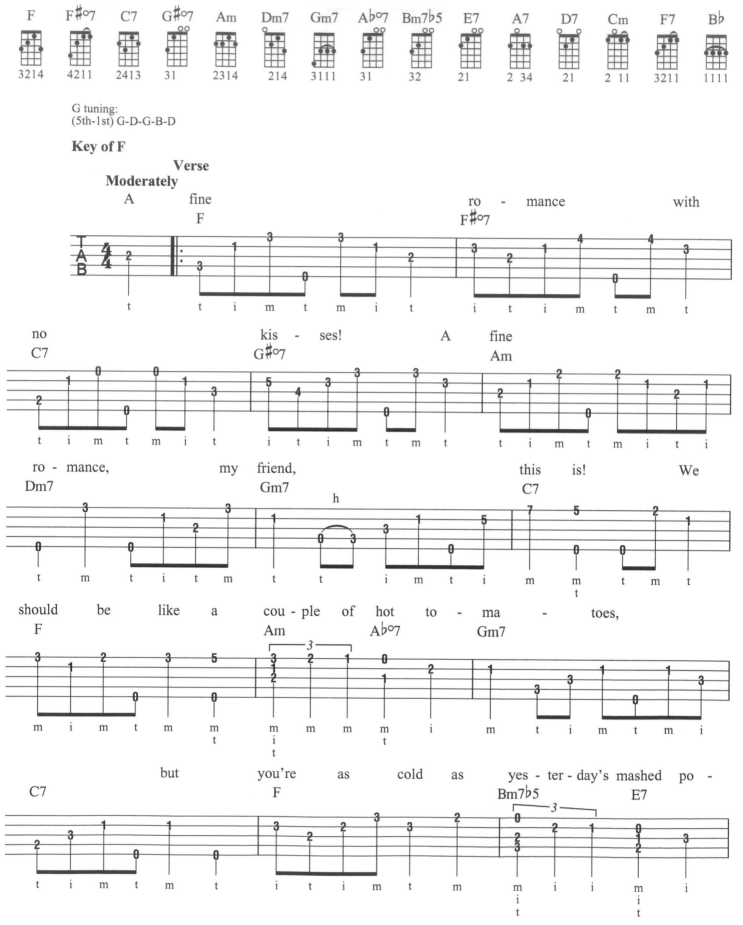

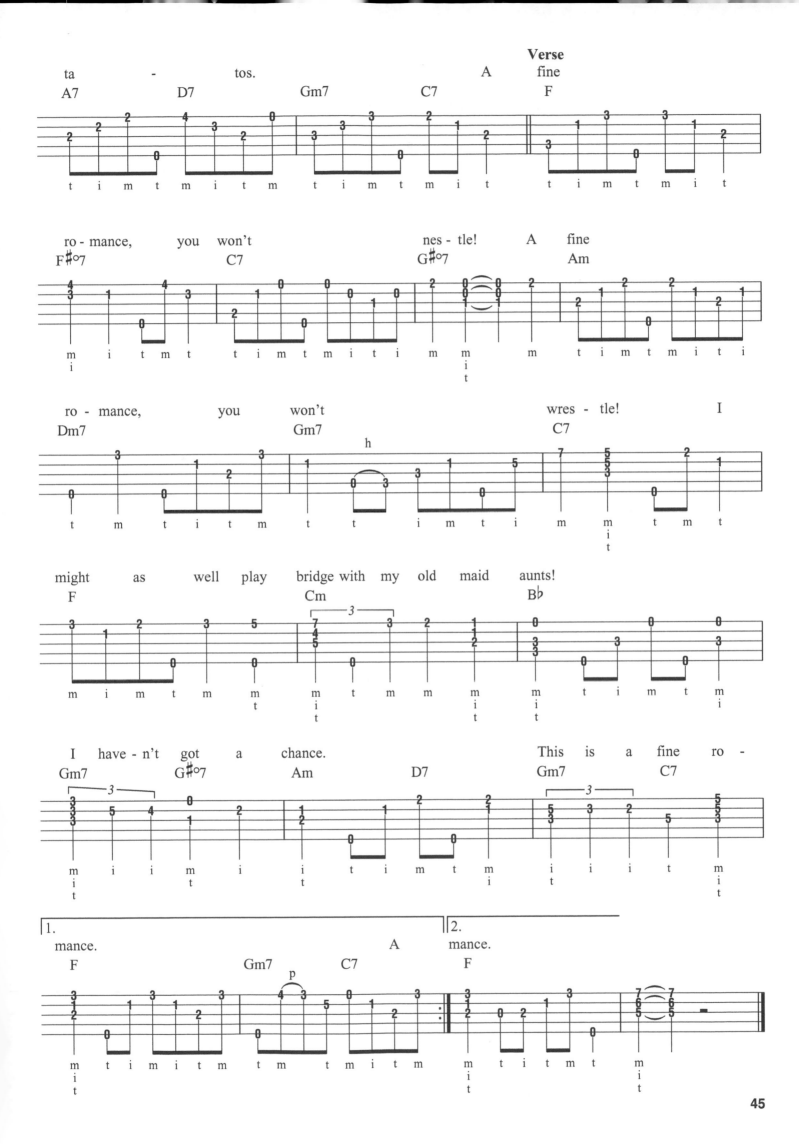

# Five Foot Two, Eyes of Blue

## (Has Anybody Seen My Girl?)

Words by Joe Young and Sam Lewis
Music by Ray Henderson

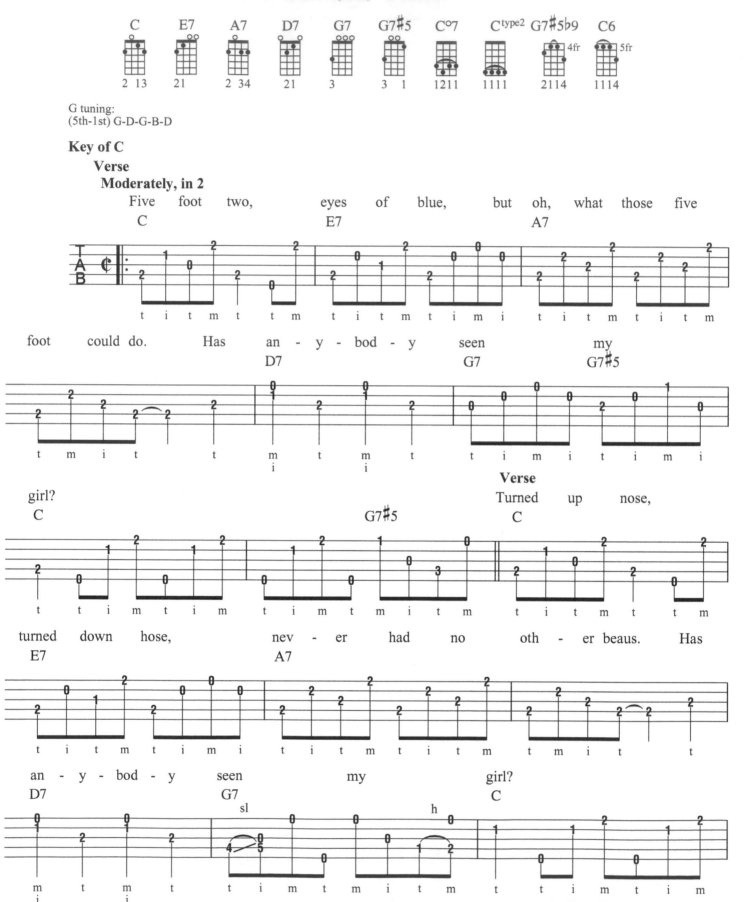

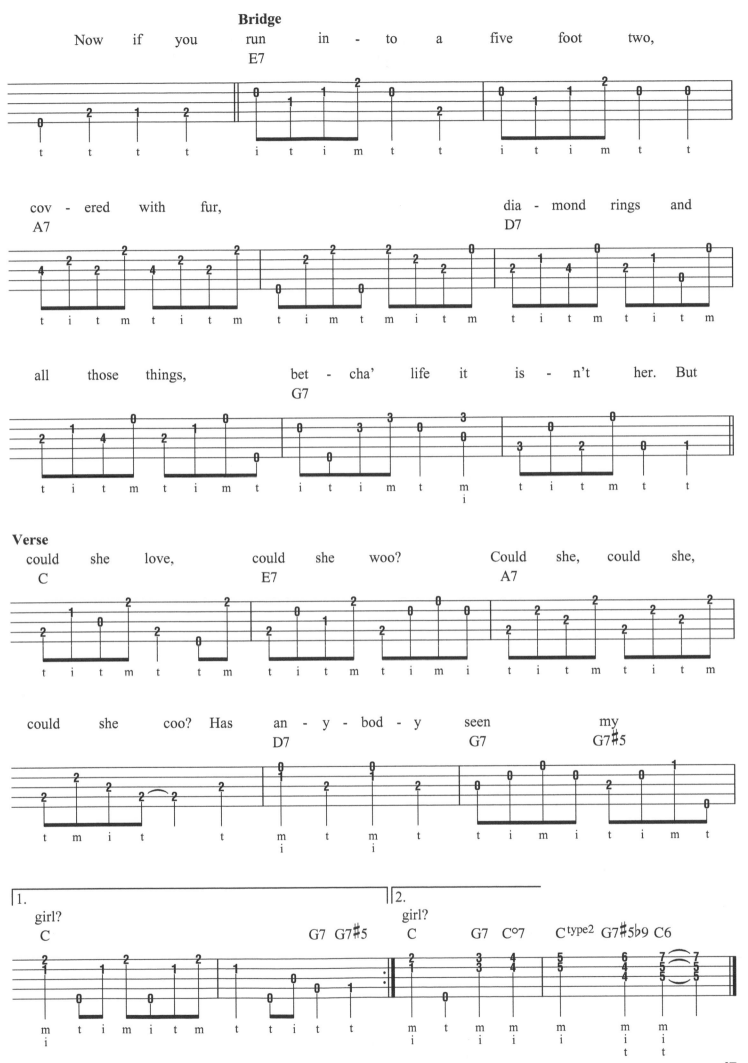

# Fly Me to the Moon
## (In Other Words)

featured in the Motion Picture ONCE AROUND
**Words and Music by Bart Howard**

C tuning:
(5th-1st) G-C-G-B-D

**Key of C**
**Verse**
**Slow & free**

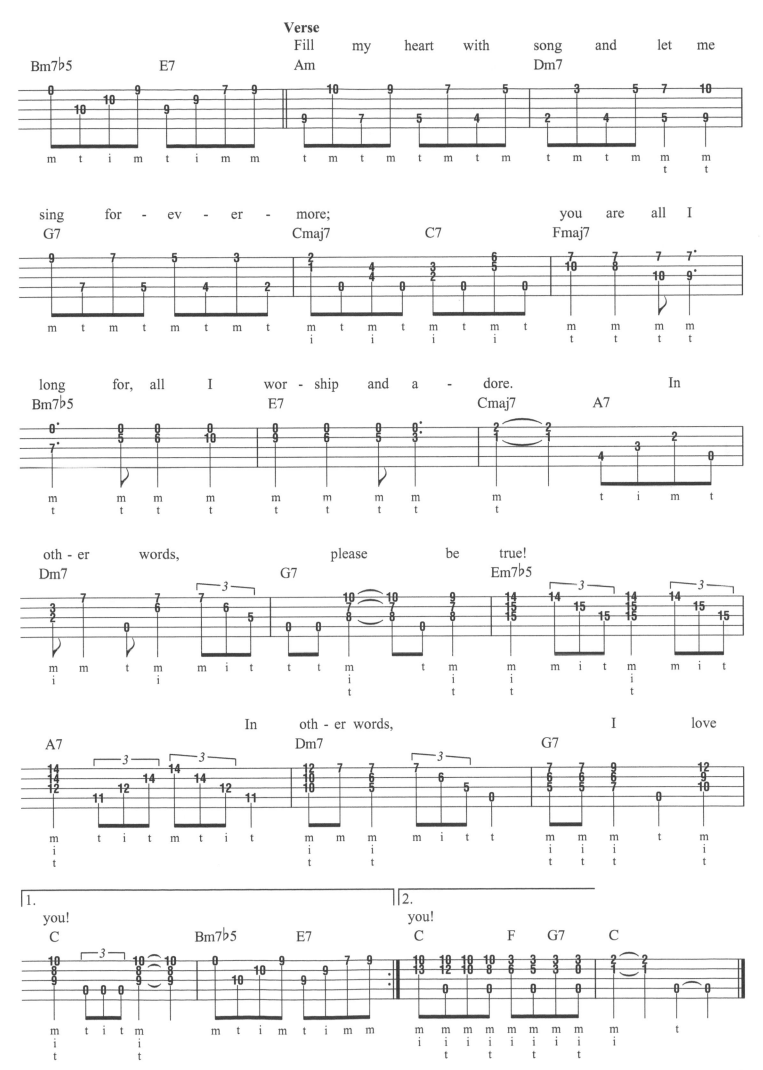

# For Me and My Gal

Words by Edgar Leslie and E. Ray Goetz
Music by George W. Meyer

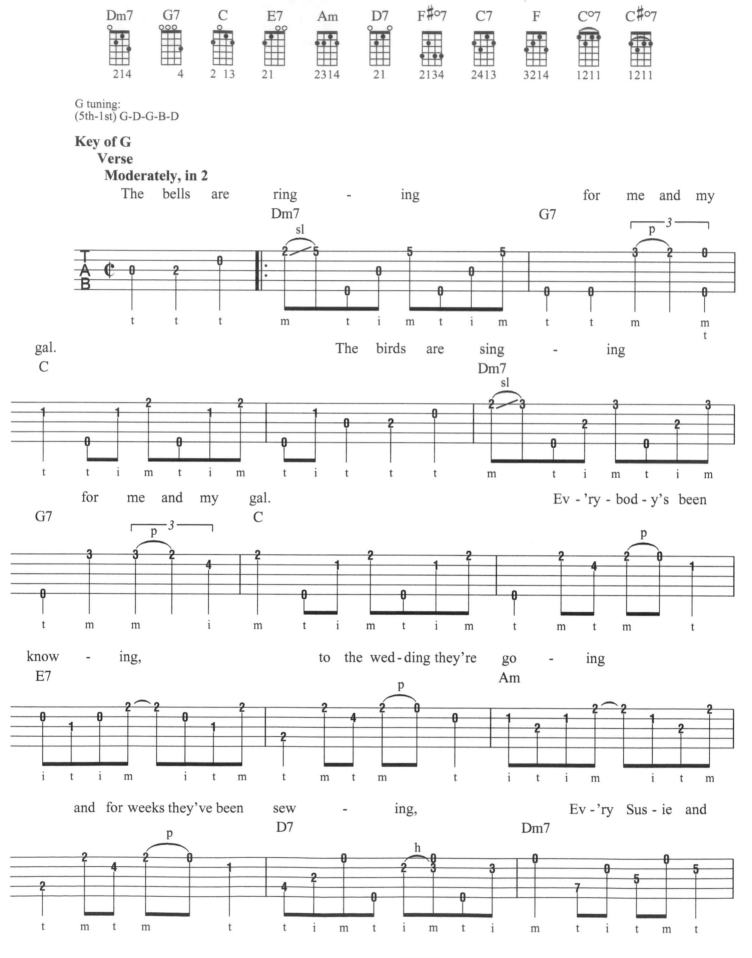

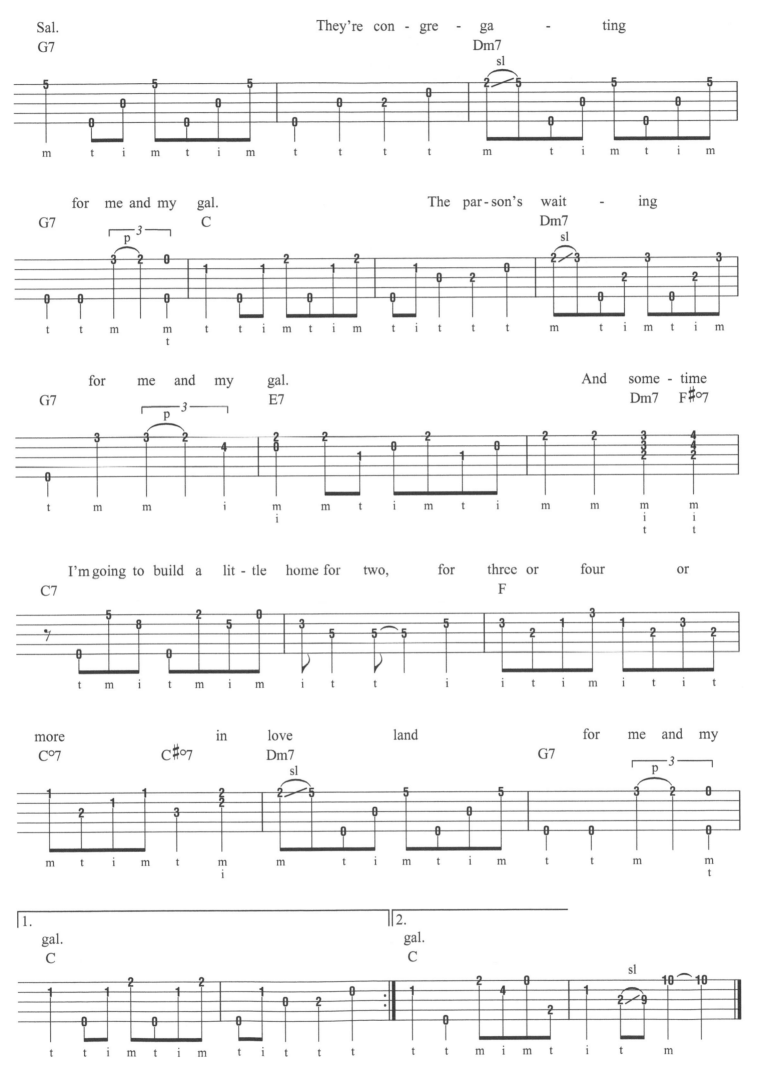

# Georgia on My Mind

**Words by Stuart Gorrell**
**Music by Hoagy Carmichael**

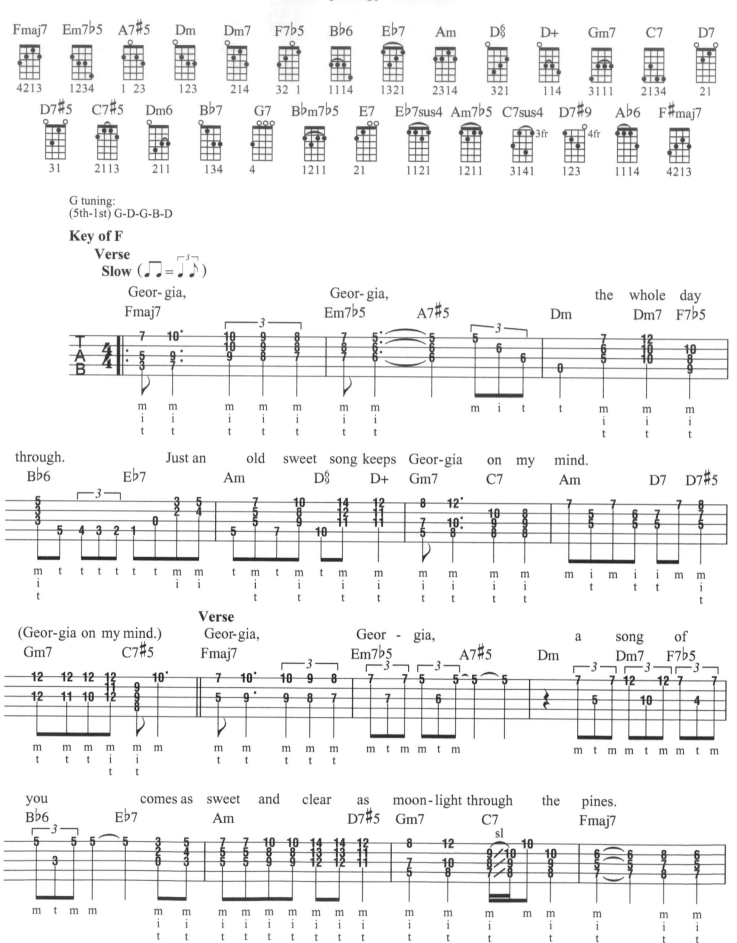

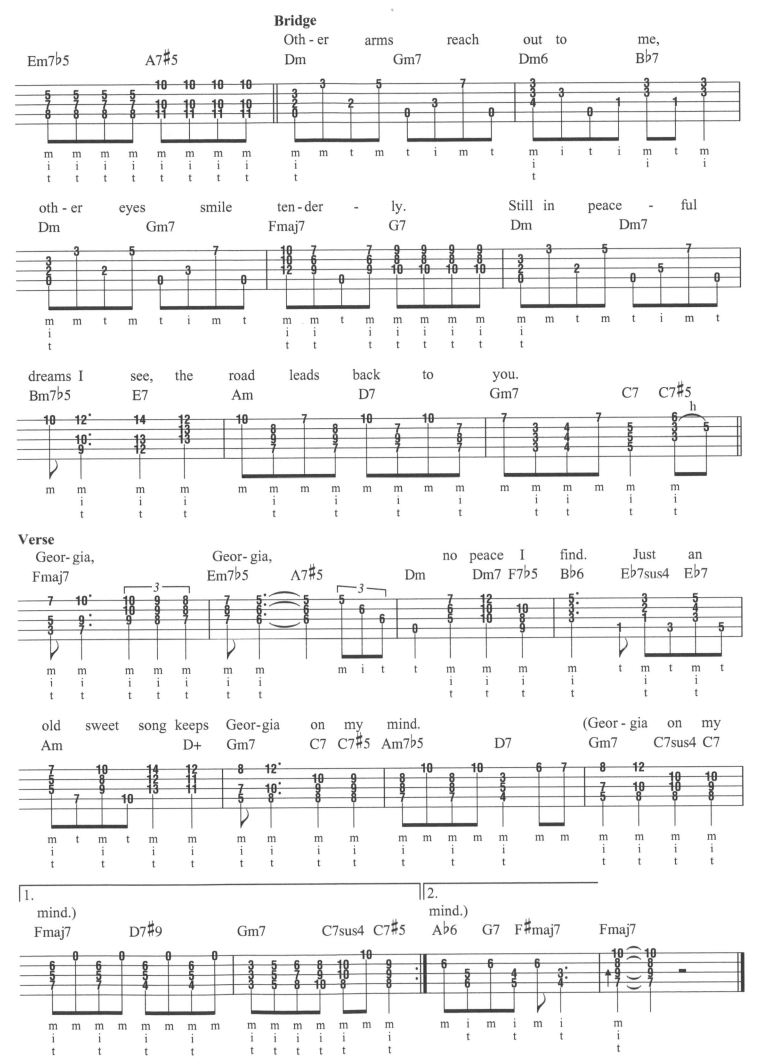

# The Glory of Love

### featured in GUESS WHO'S COMING TO DINNER
### Words and Music by Billy Hill

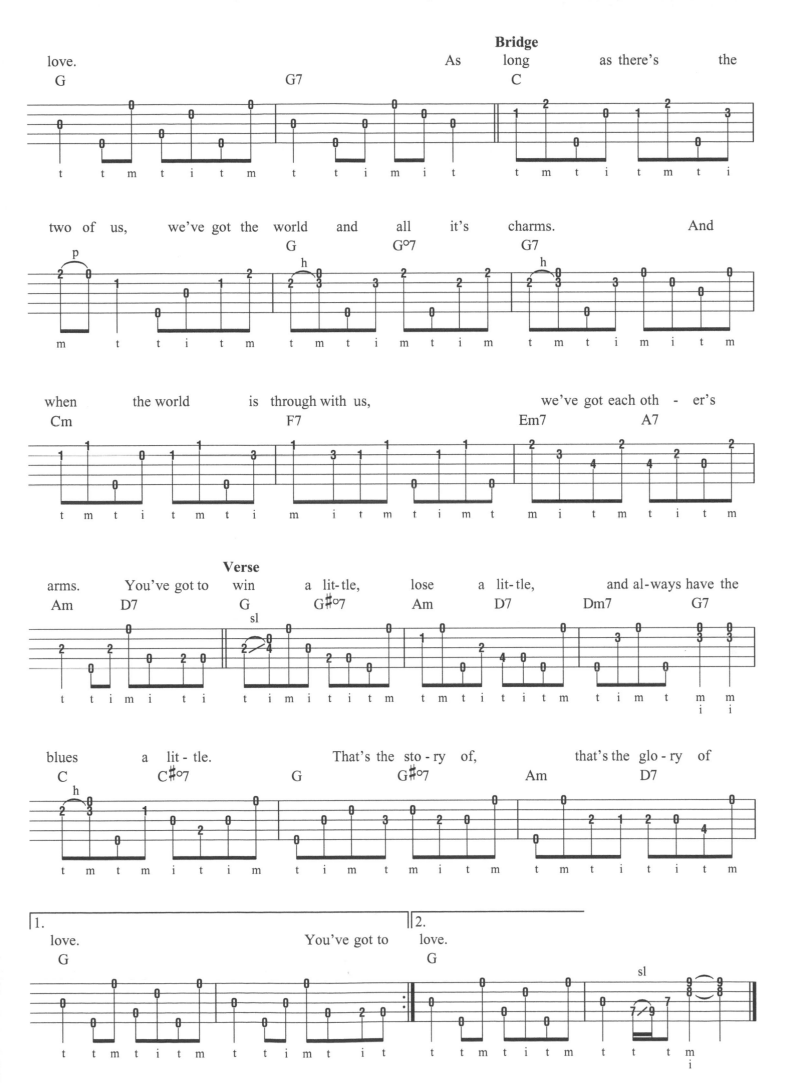

# Heartaches

**Words by John Klenner**
**Music by Al Hoffman**

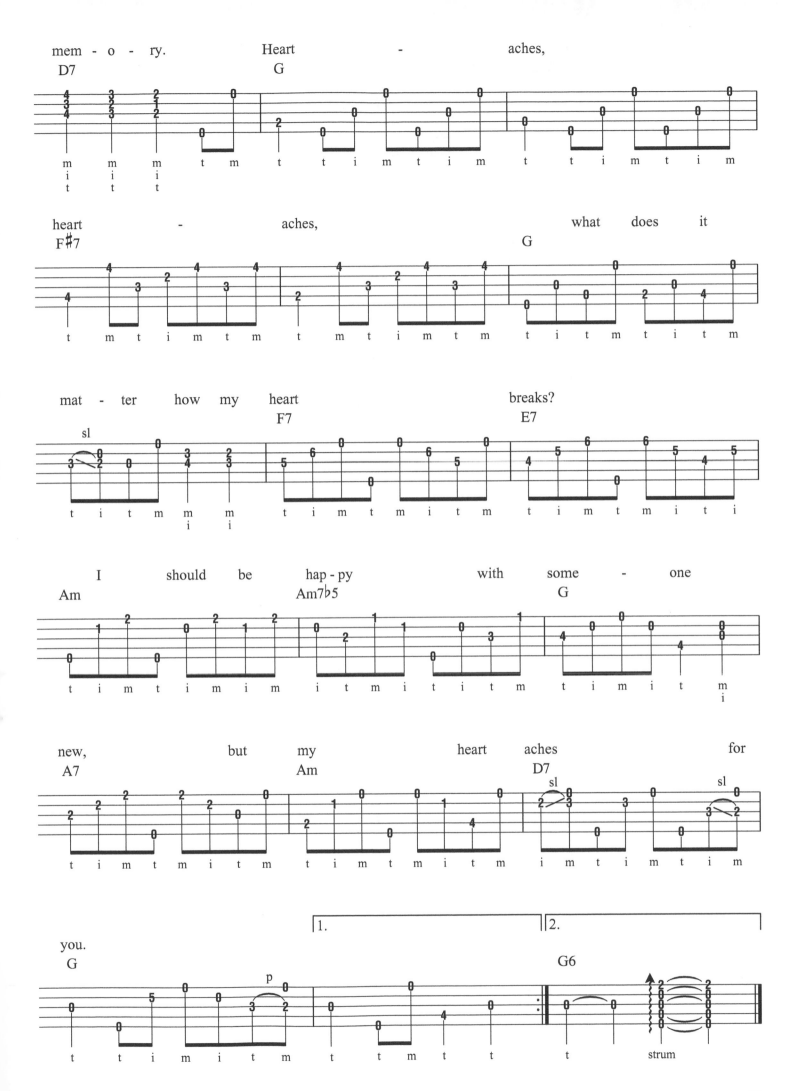

# Home on the Range

**Lyrics by Dr. Brewster Higley**
**Music by Dan Kelly**

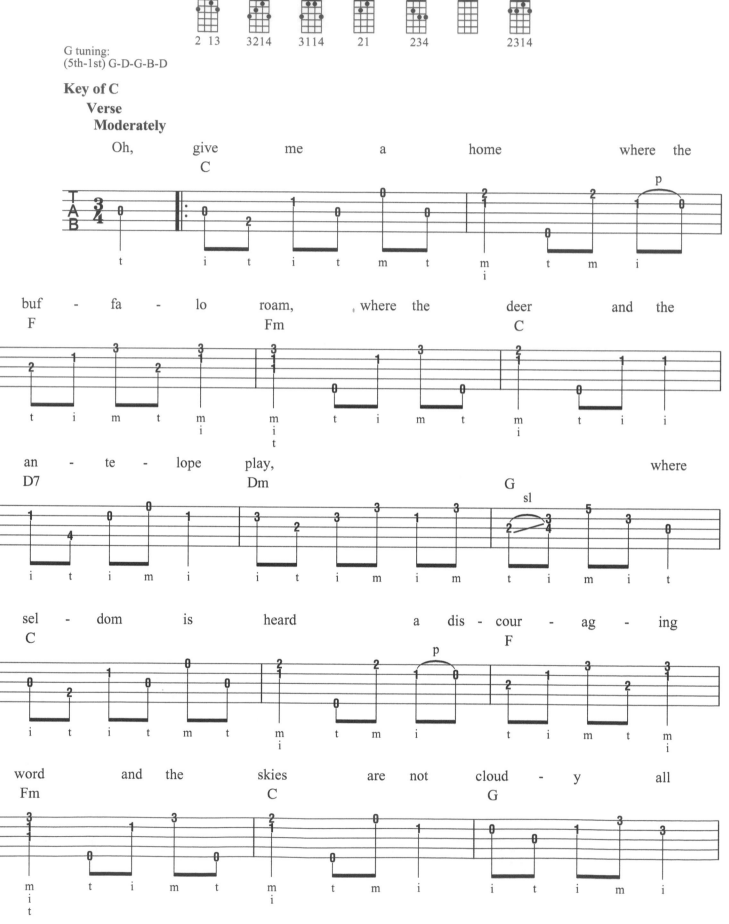

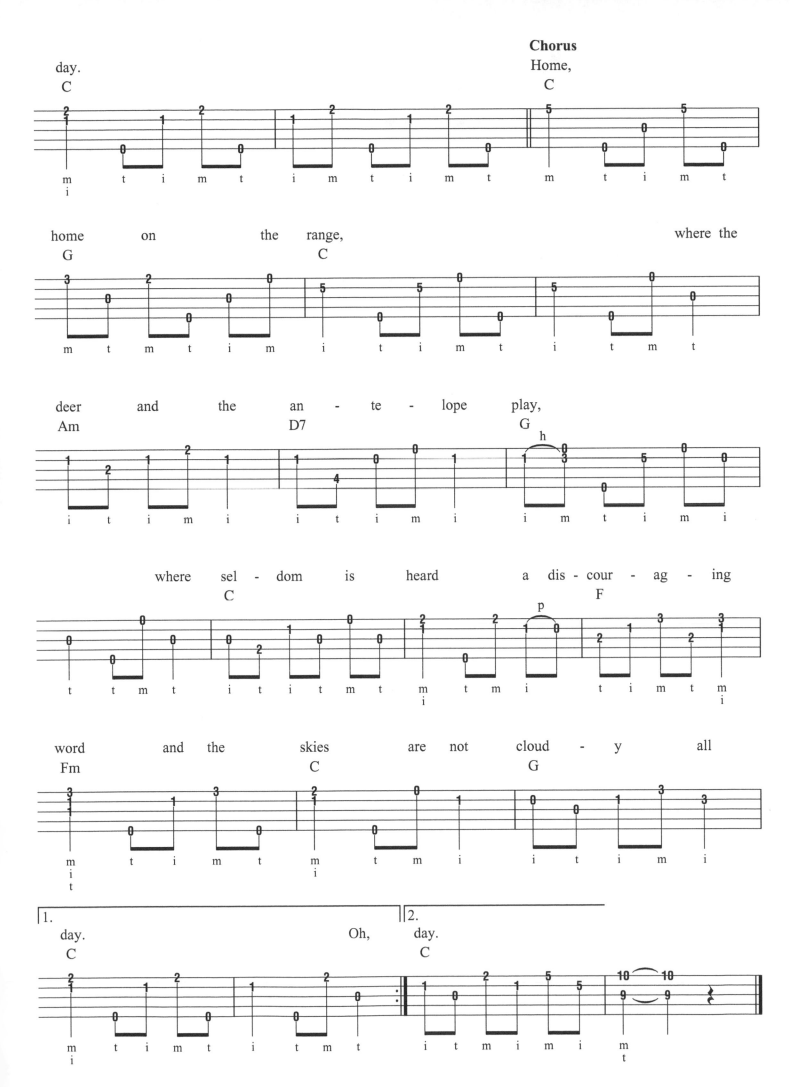

# Honeysuckle Rose

from AIN'T MISBEHAVIN'
Words by Andy Razaf
Music by Thomas "Fats" Waller

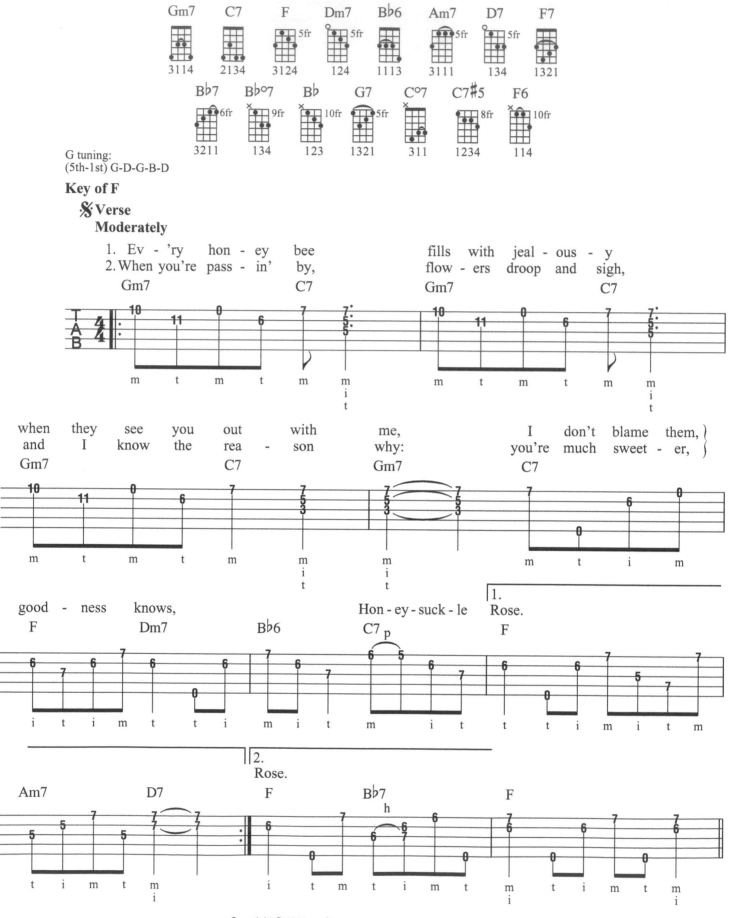

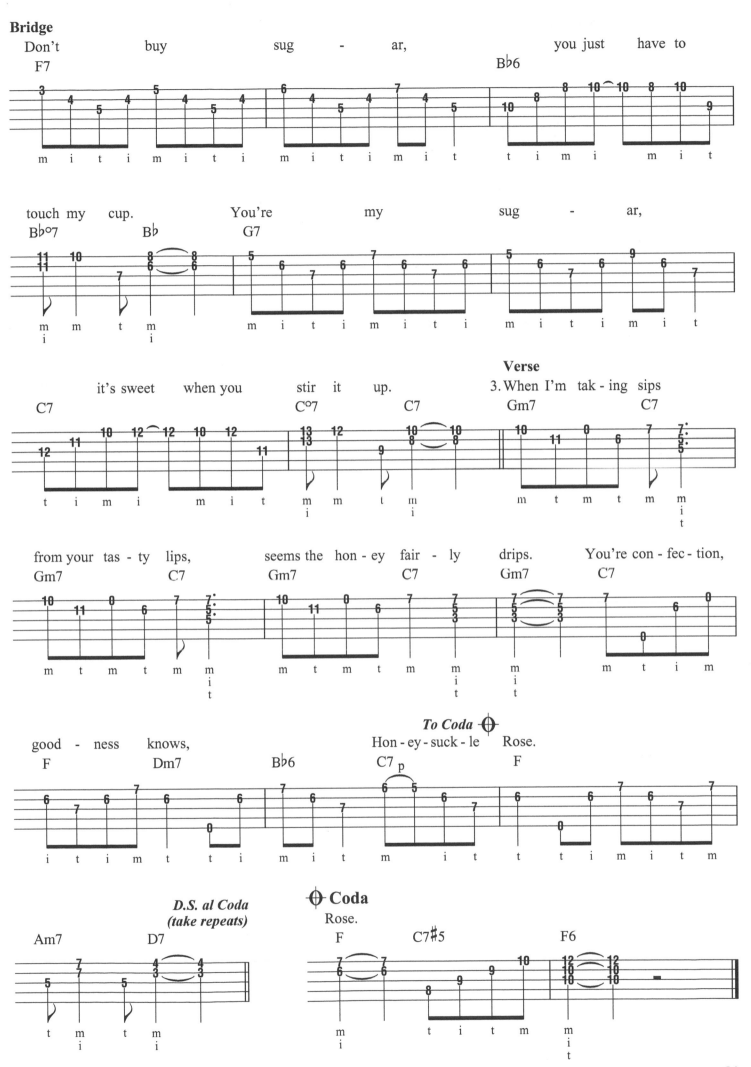

# I Can't Give You Anything but Love

### from BLACKBIRDS OF 1928
### Words and Music by Jimmy McHugh and Dorothy Fields

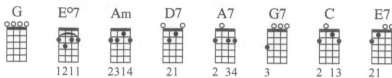

G tuning:
(5th-1st) G-D-G-B-D

**Key of G**

**Verse**
**Moderately**

I can't give you an - y - thing but love,

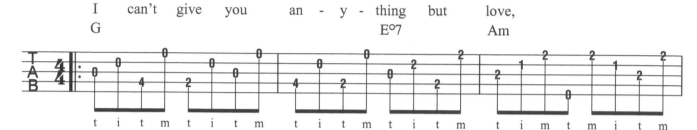

ba - by, that's the on - ly thing I've plen - ty

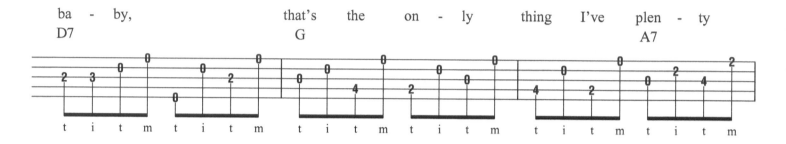

of, ba - by. Dream a while,

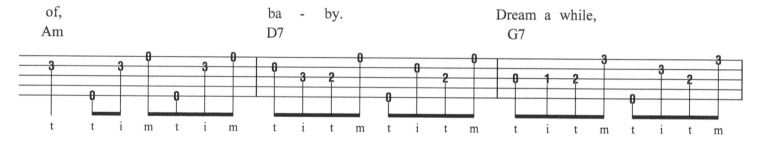

scheme a while, we're sure to find

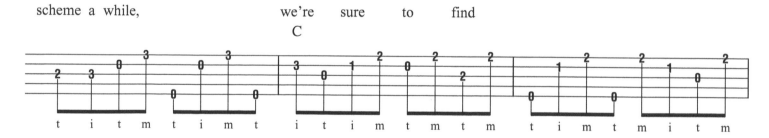

hap - pi - ness and I guess all those things you've

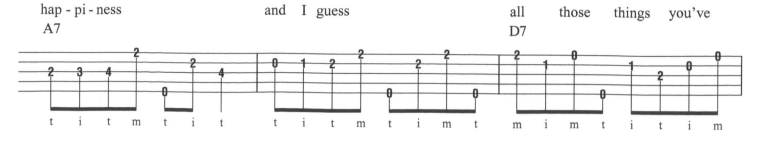

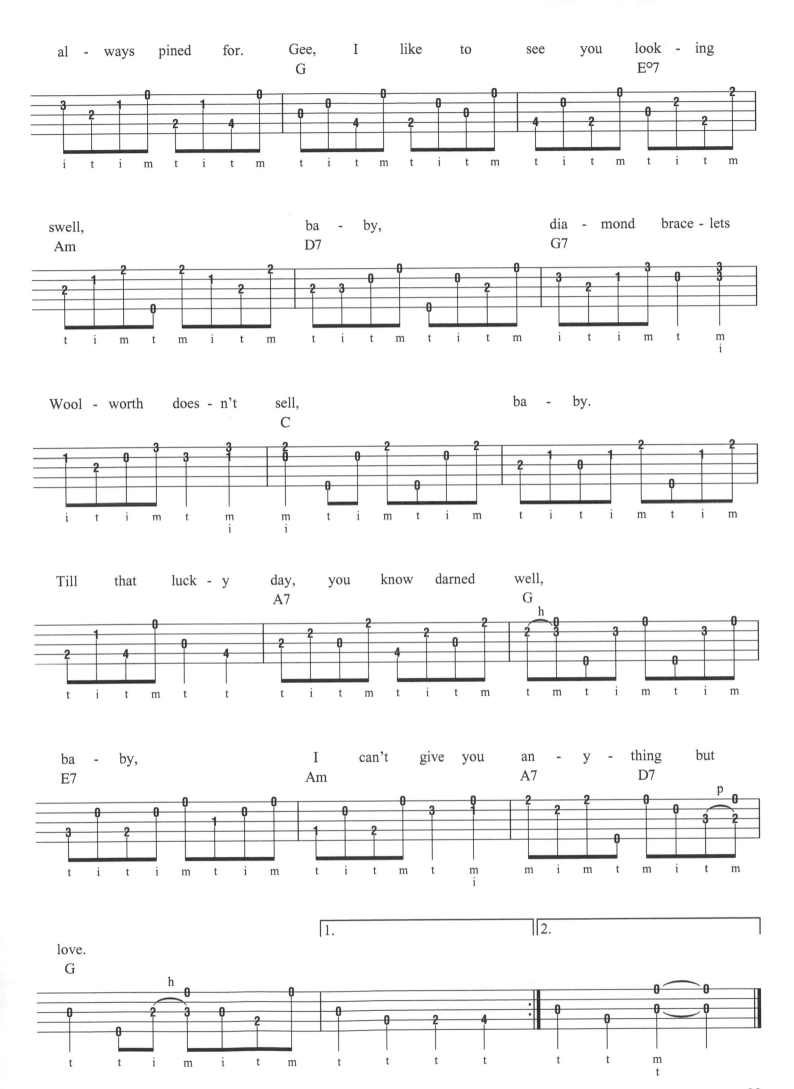

# I Could Have Danced All Night

from MY FAIR LADY
**Words by Alan Jay Lerner**
**Music by Frederick Loewe**

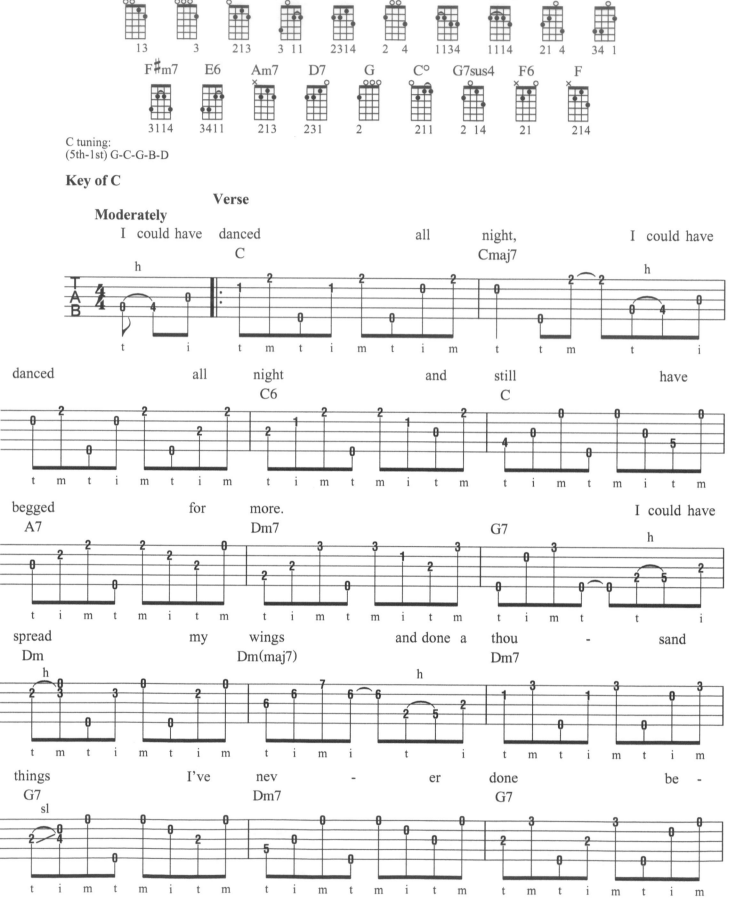

C tuning:
(5th-1st) G-C-G-B-D

**Key of C**

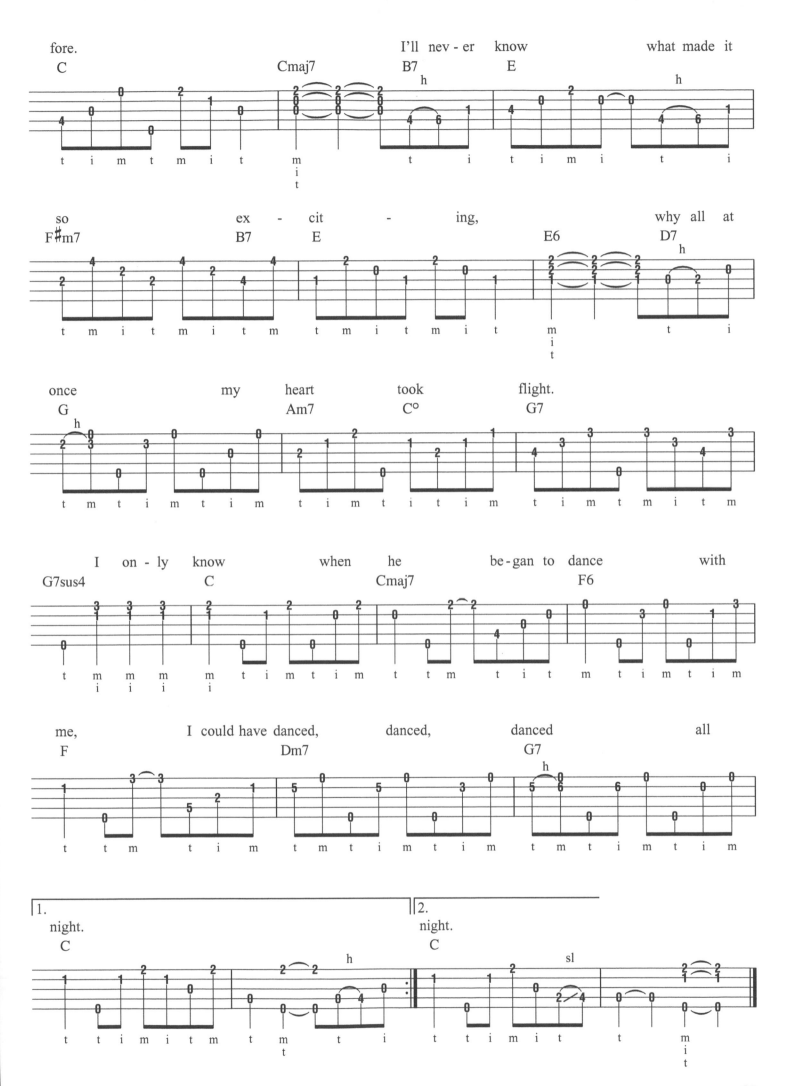

# I Want to Be a Cowboy's Sweetheart

**Words and Music by Patsy Montana**

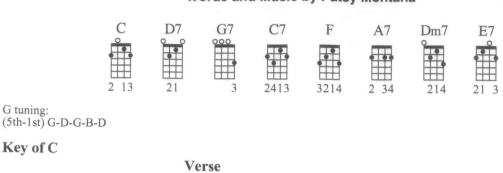

G tuning:
(5th-1st) G-D-G-B-D

**Key of C**

**Verse**

**Fast, in 2**

I want to be      a    cow - boy's

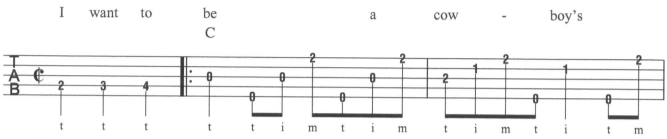

sweet - heart,      I    want to learn    to

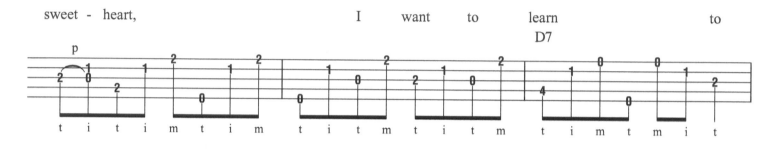

rope    and    ride      I   want to

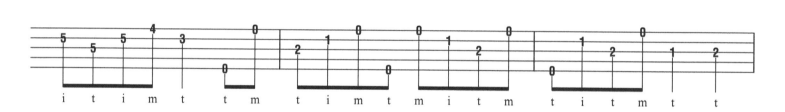

ride   o'er the   plains   and   the   des - ert

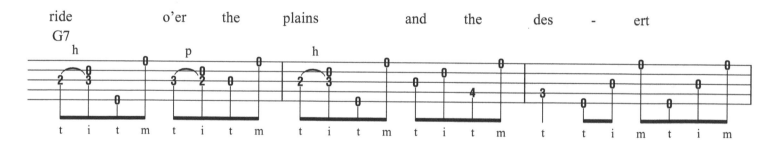

out    west    of   the   Great      Di -

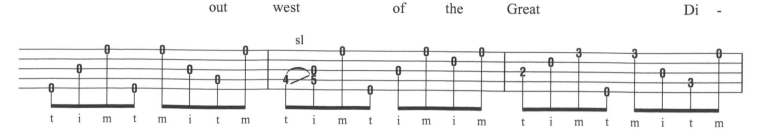

66

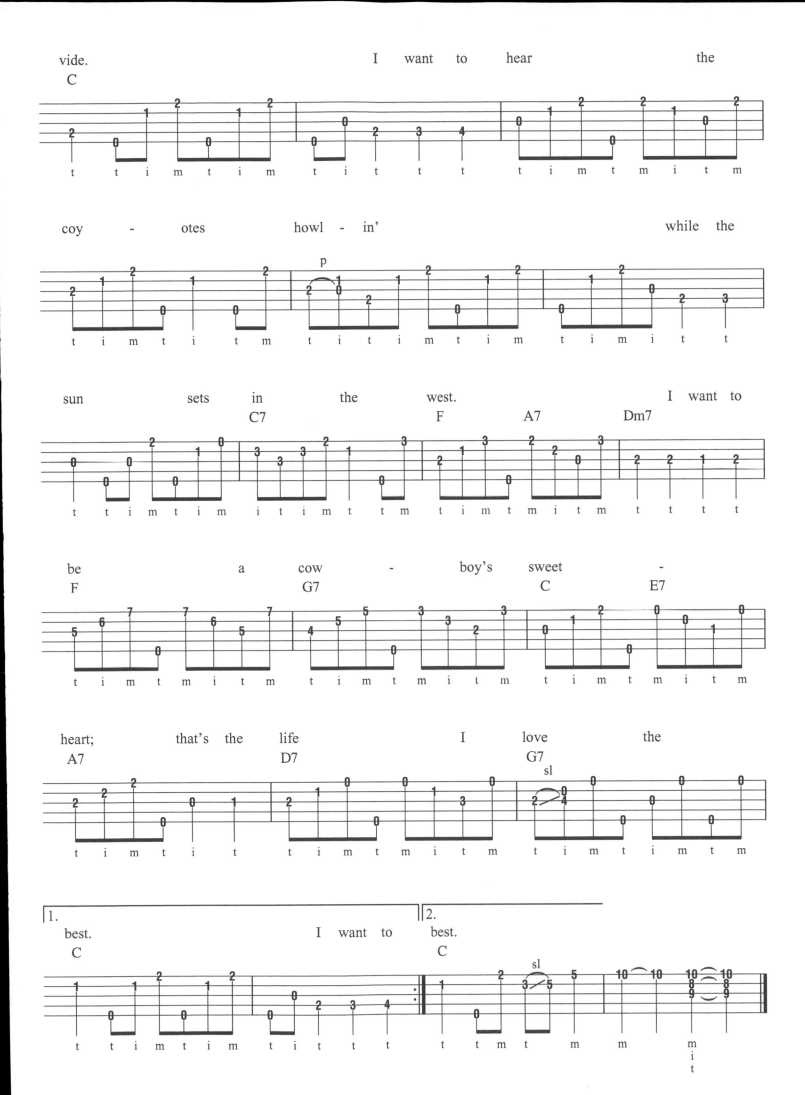

# I'll See You in My Dreams

**Words by Gus Kahn**
**Music by Isham Jones**

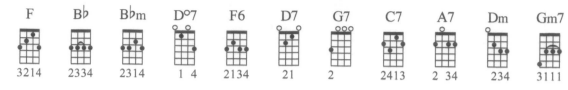

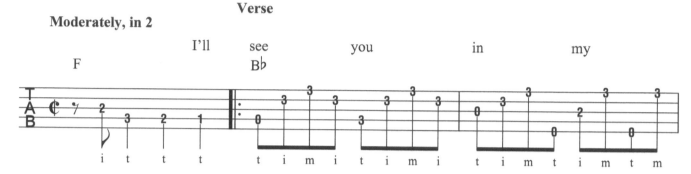

G tuning:
(5th-1st) G-D-G-B-D

**Key of F**

**Verse**

**Moderately, in 2**

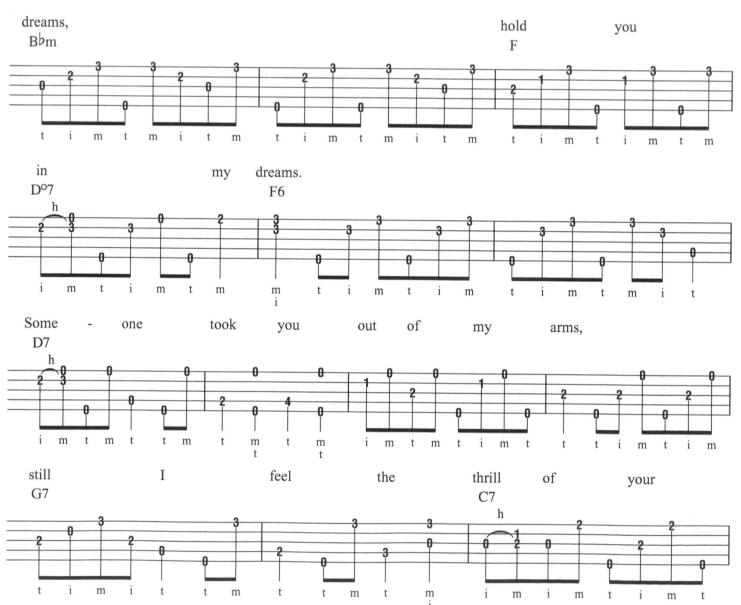

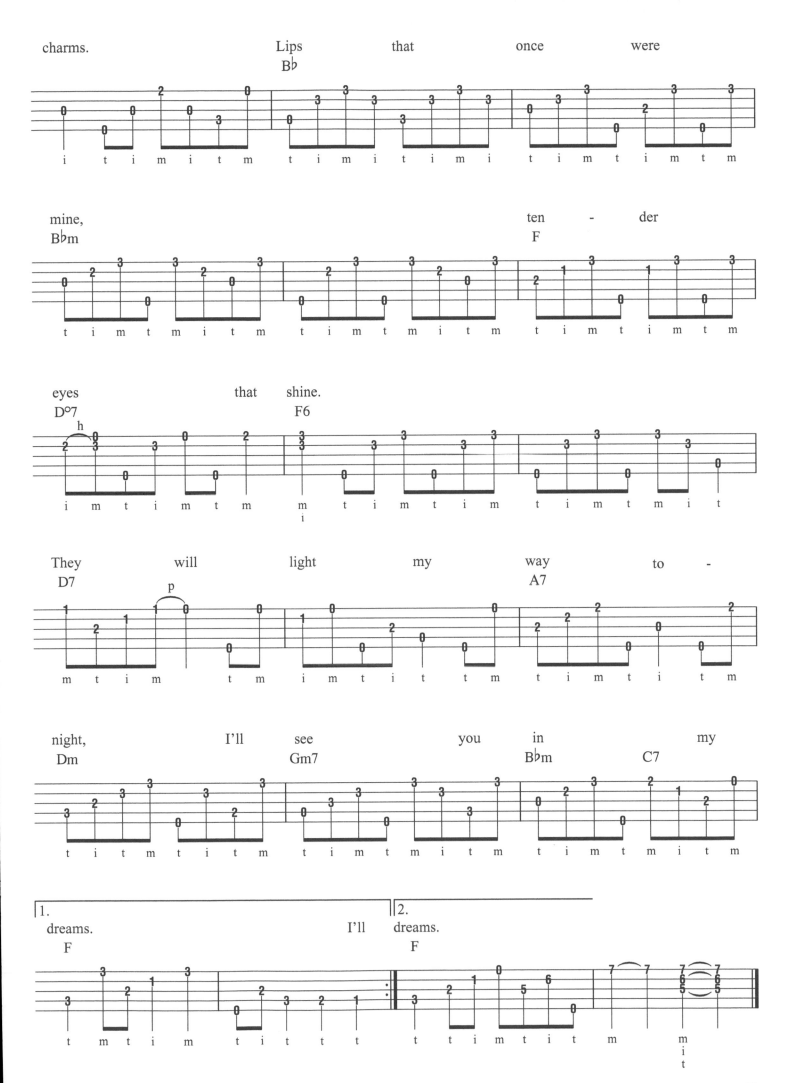

# I'm Always Chasing Rainbows

**Words by Joseph McCarthy**
**Music by Harry Carroll**

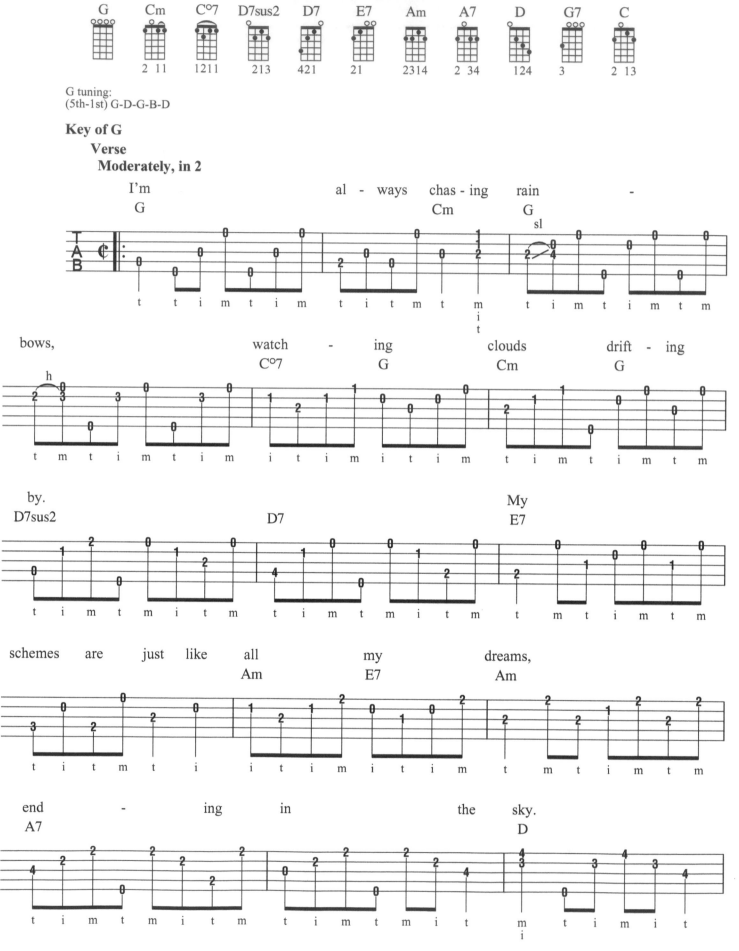

G tuning:
(5th-1st) G-D-G-B-D

**Key of G**
**Verse**
**Moderately, in 2**

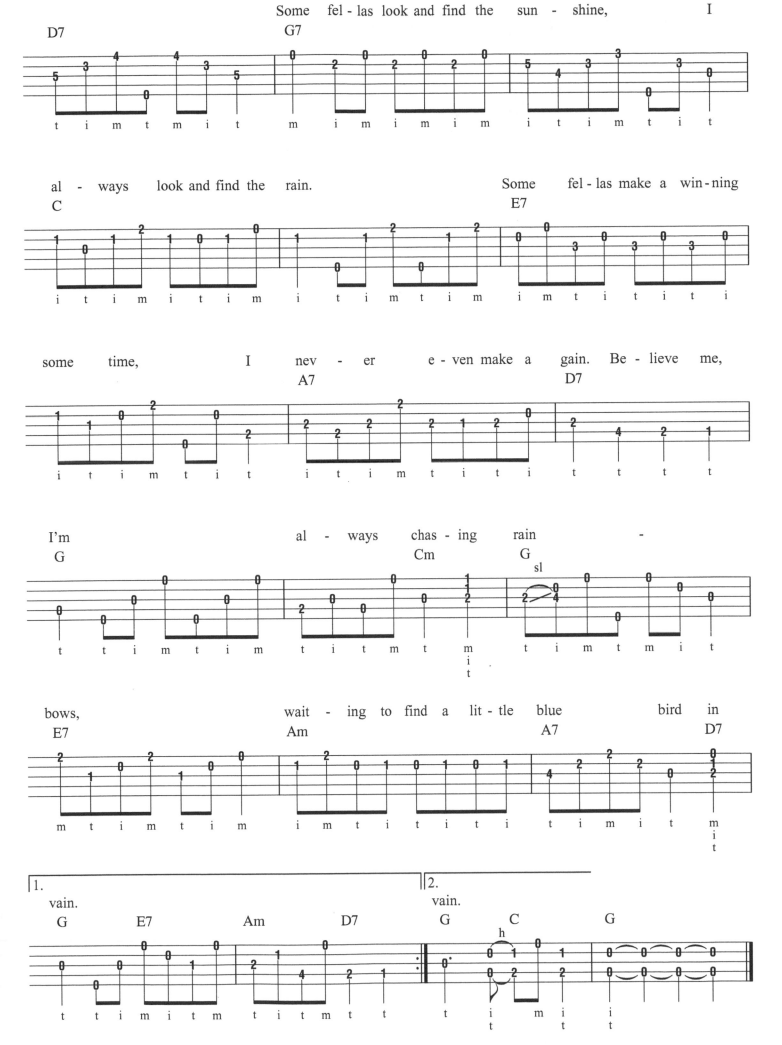

# I'm Looking Over a Four Leaf Clover

**Words by Mort Dixon**
**Music by Harry Woods**

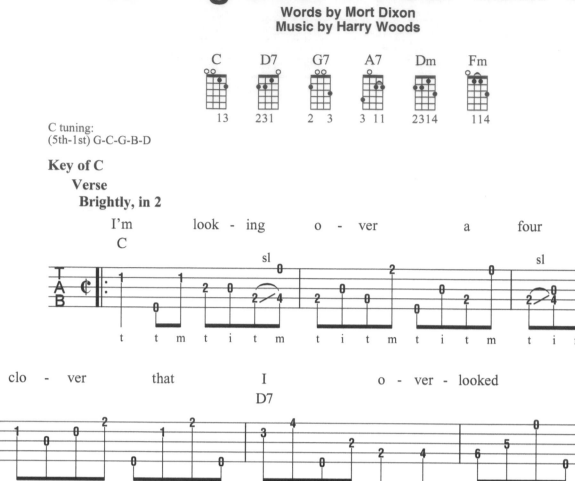

C tuning:
(5th-1st) G-C-G-B-D

**Key of C**
   **Verse**
     **Brightly, in 2**

I'm    look - ing    o - ver    a    four    leaf

clo - ver    that    I    o - ver - looked    be -

fore;    one    leaf    is

sun - shine,    the    sec - ond    is    rain,

third    is    the    ros - es    that    grow    in    the

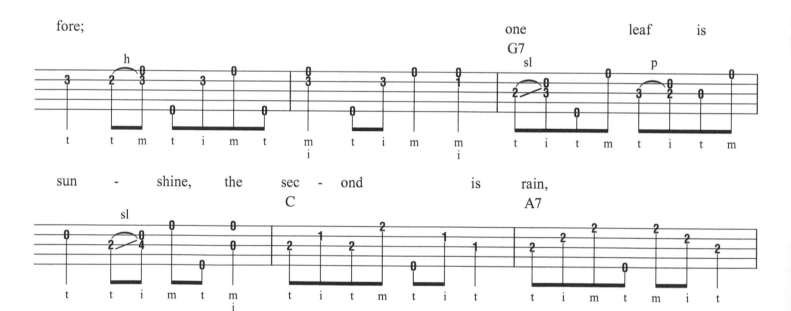

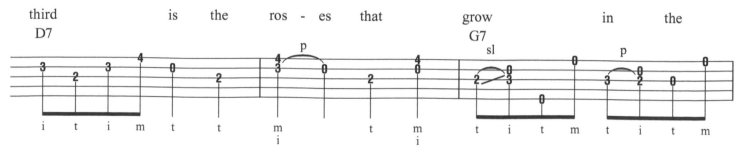

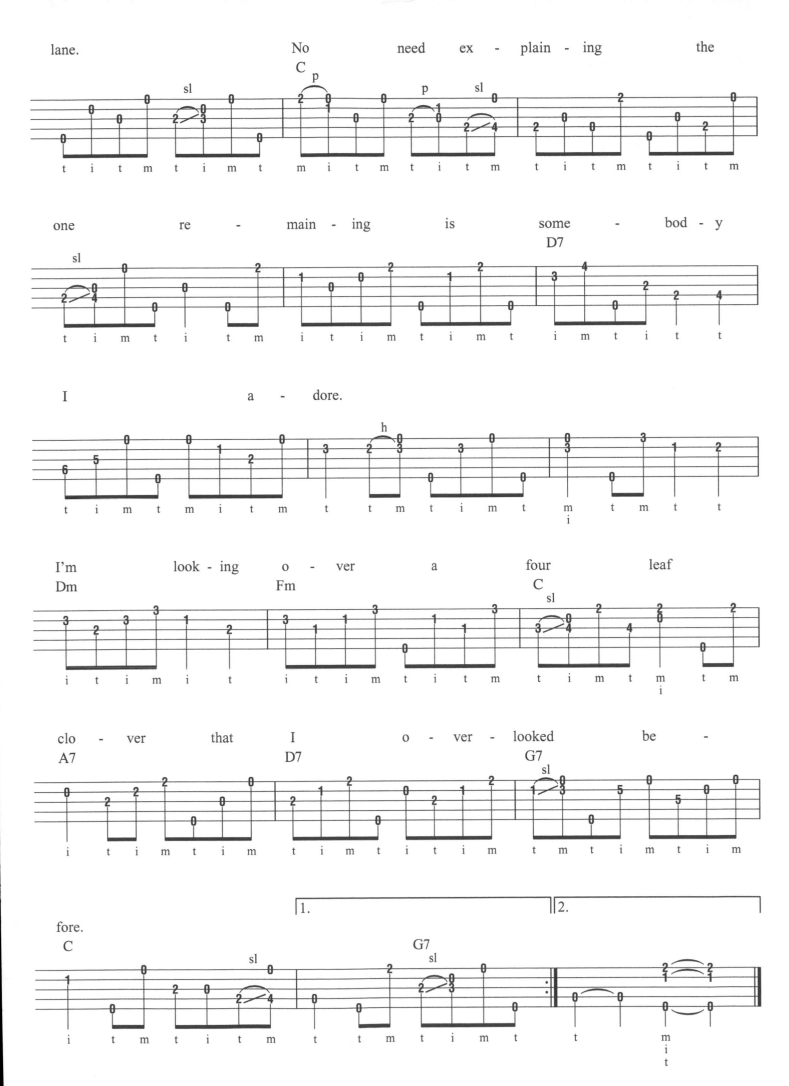

# If You Knew Susie (Like I Know Susie)

Words and Music by B.G. DeSylva and Joseph Meyer

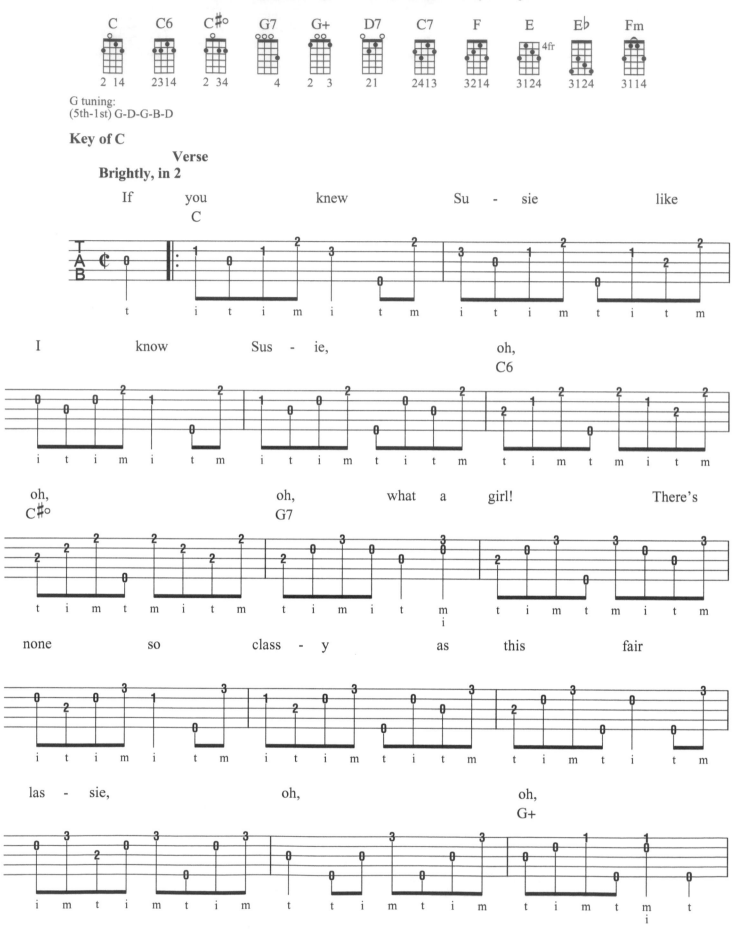

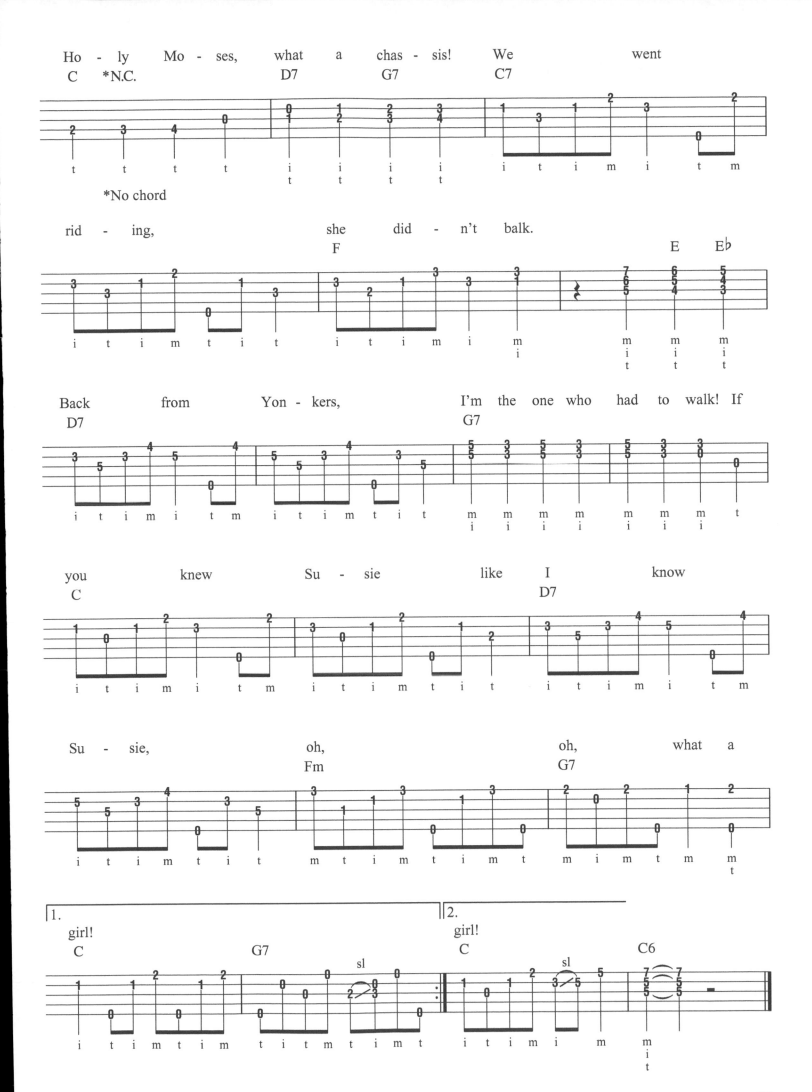

# In a Shanty in Old Shanty Town

**Lyric by Joe Young**
**Music by Jack Little and Ira Schuster**

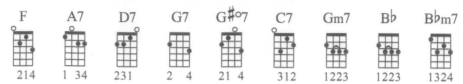

C tuning:
(5th-1st) G-C-G-B-D

**Key of F**

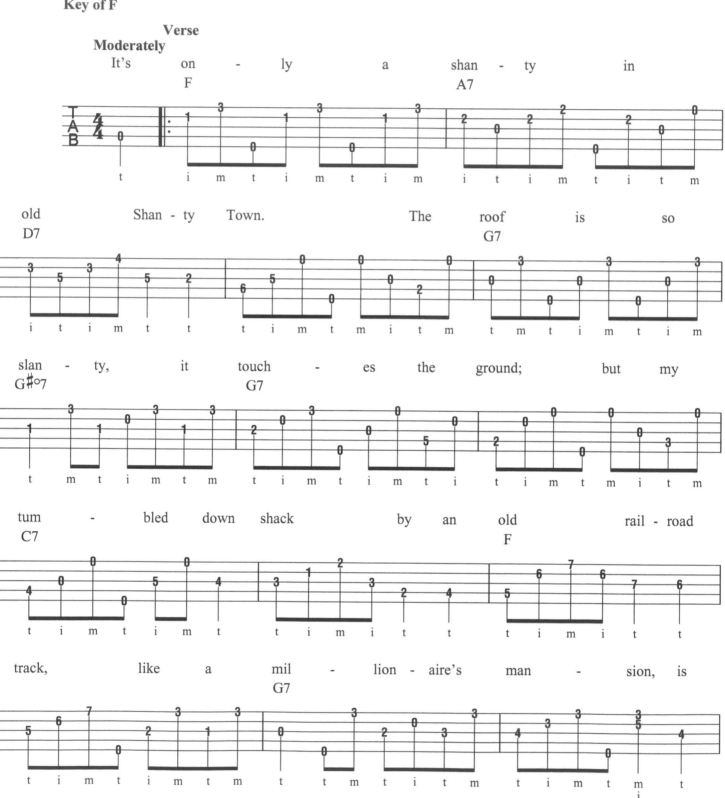

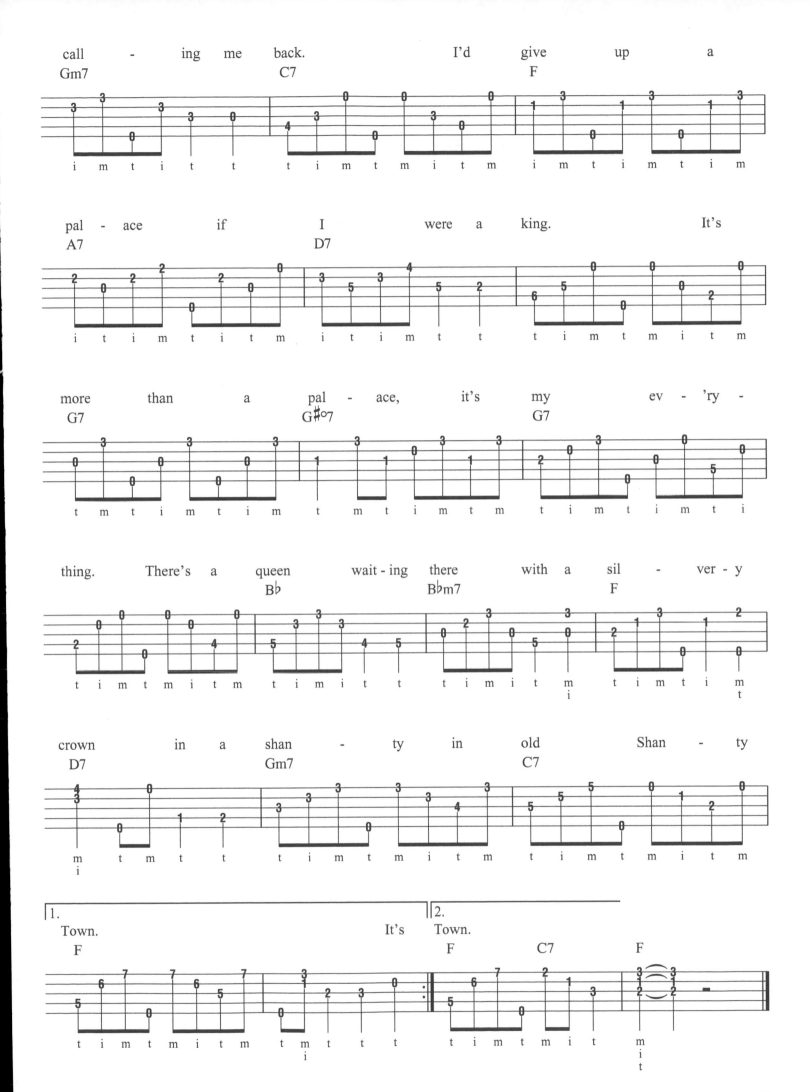

# It Had to Be You

**Words by Gus Kahn**
**Music by Isham Jones**

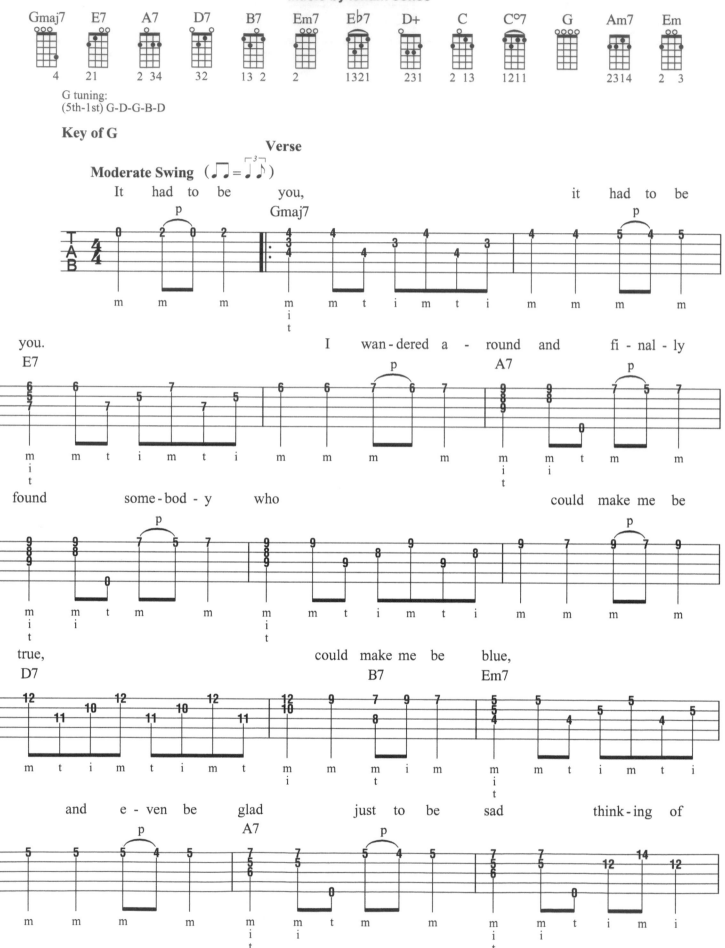

# It's a Sin to Tell a Lie

**Words and Music by Billy Mayhew**

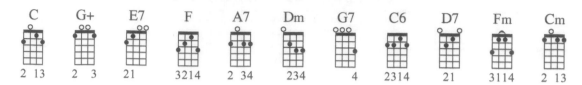

G tuning:
(5th-1st) G-D-G-B-D

**Key of C**

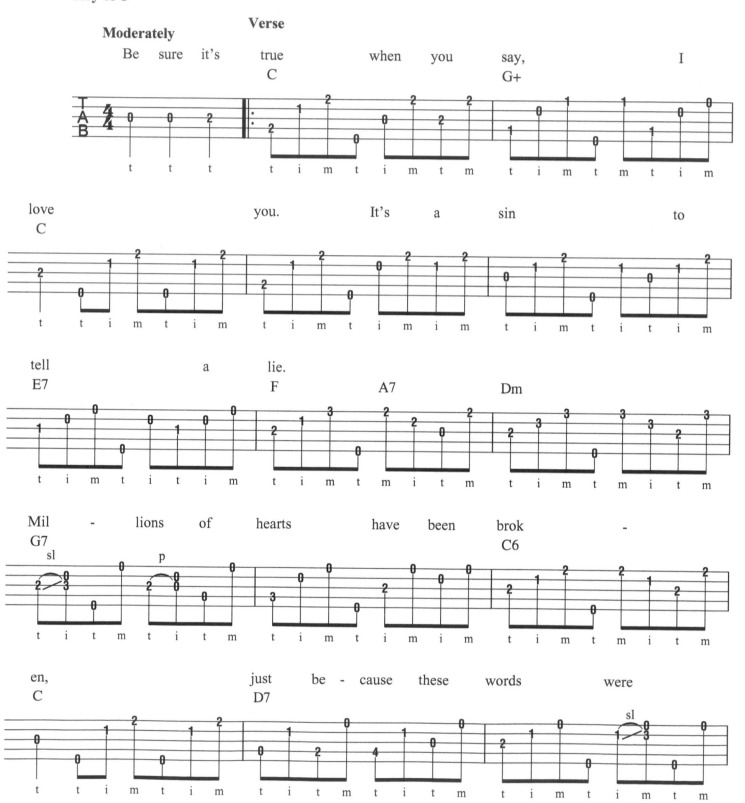

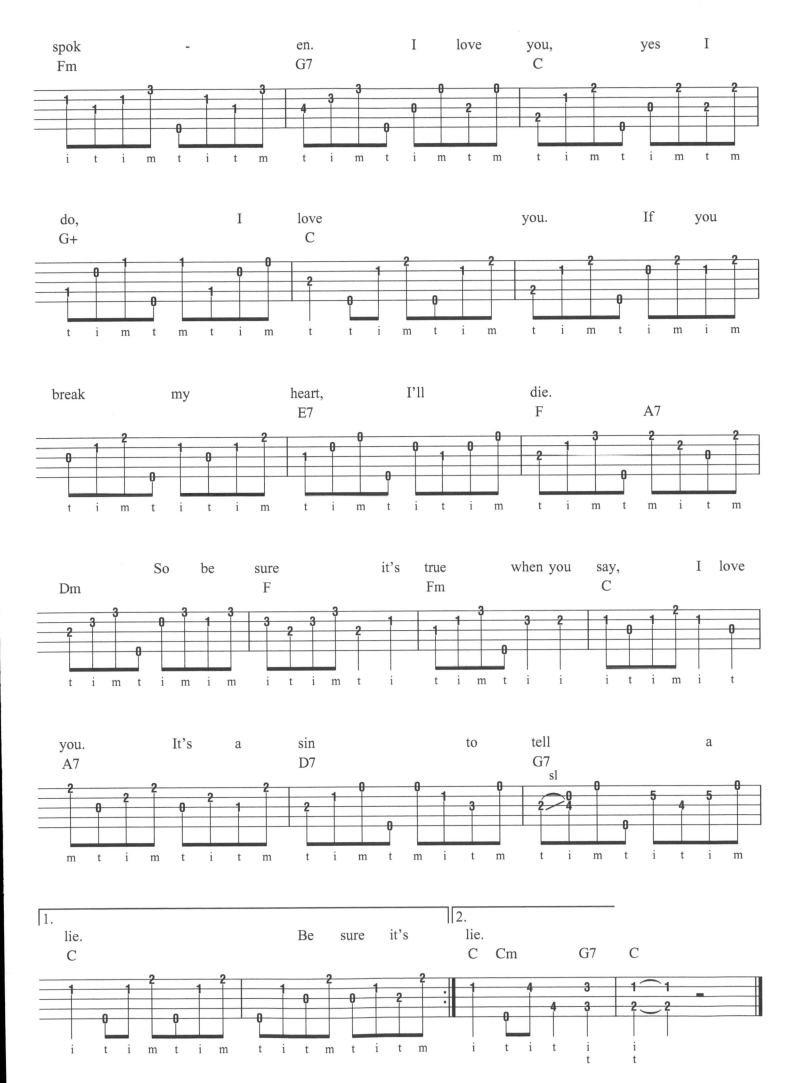

# Jingle Jangle Jingle
## (I Got Spurs)

from the Paramount Picture THE FOREST RANGERS
**Words by Frank Loesser**
**Music by Joseph J. Lilley**

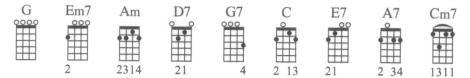

G tuning:
(5th-1st) G-D-G-B-D

**Key of G**

𝄋 **Chorus**

**Moderately, in 2**

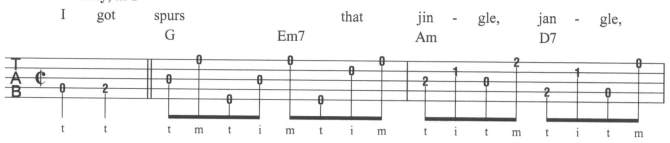

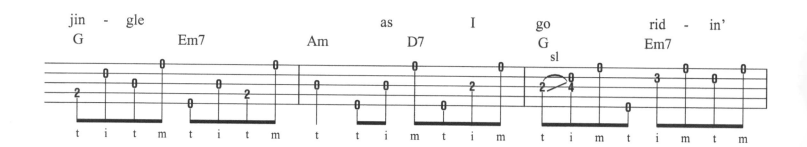

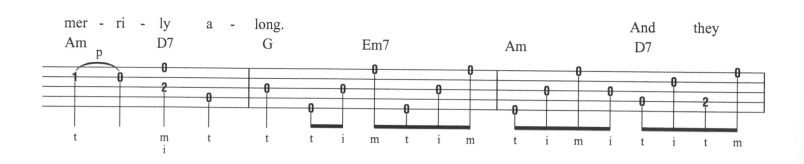

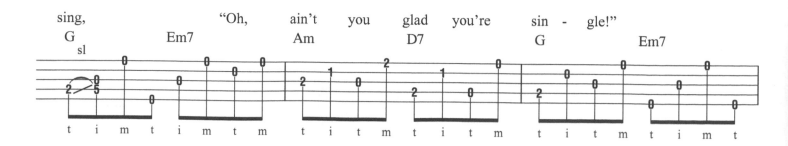

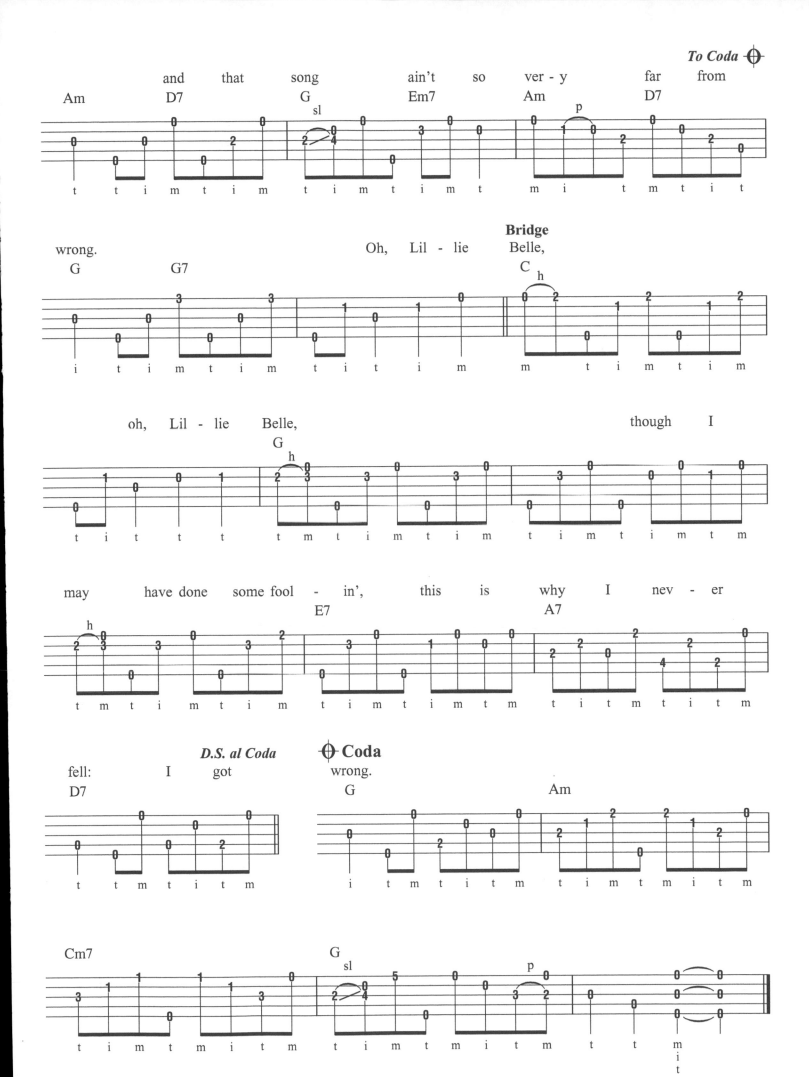

# Just Around the Corner

## Words and Music by Albert Von Tilzer and Dolph Singer

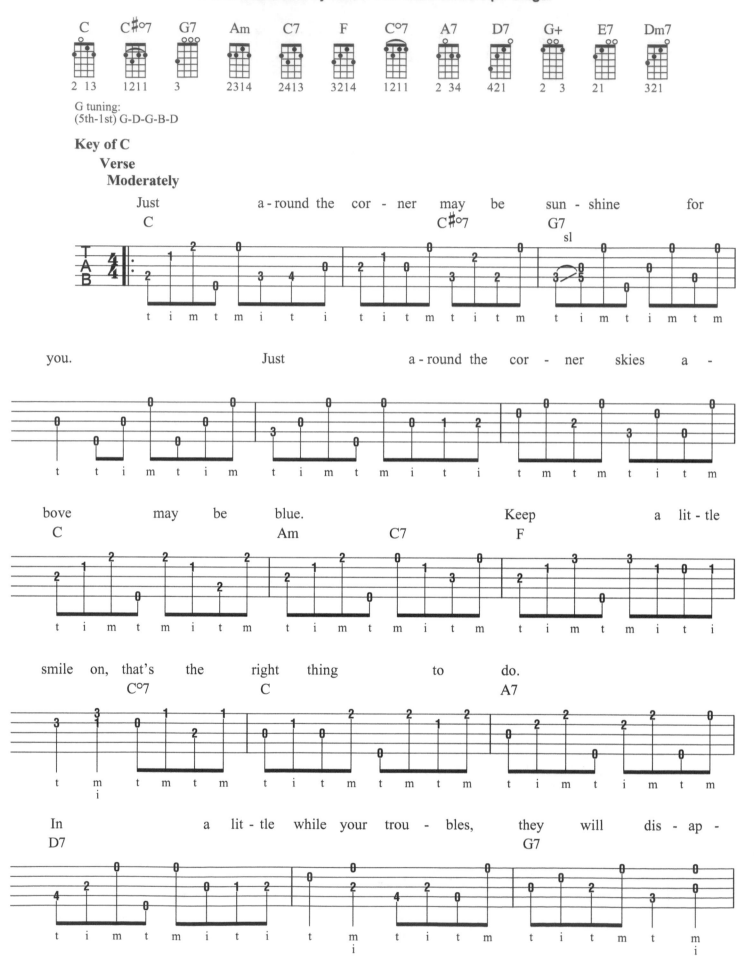

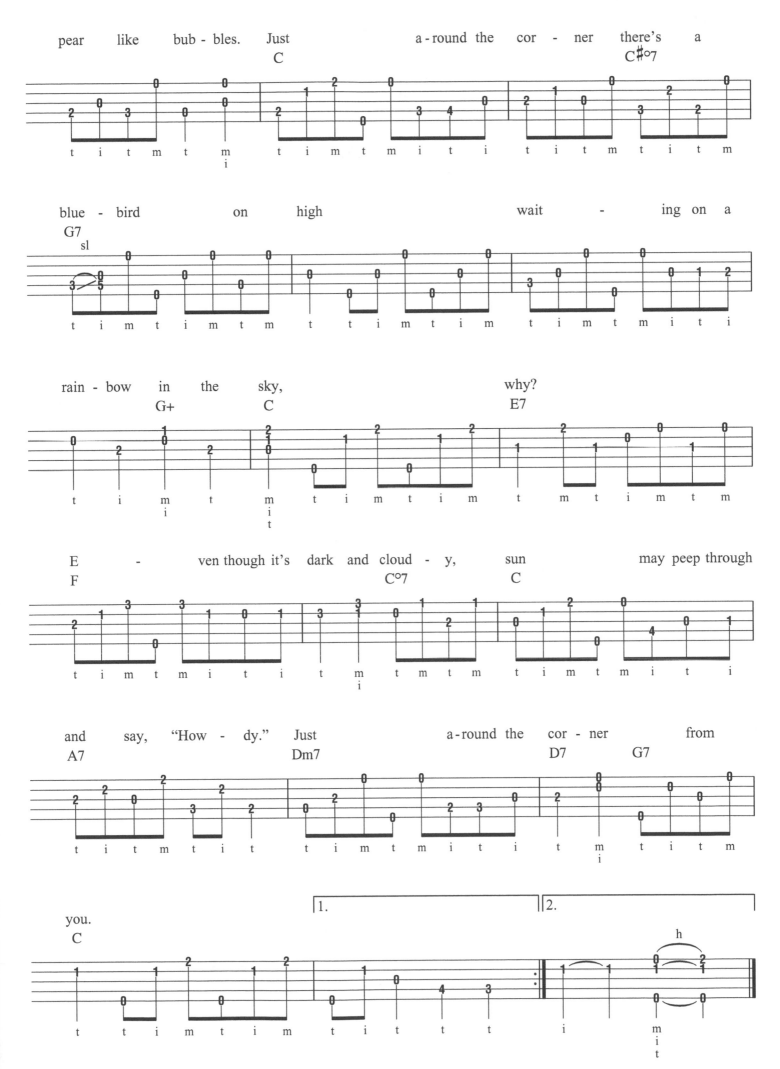

# Lazy River

### from THE BEST YEARS OF OUR LIVES
**Words and Music by Hoagy Carmichael and Sidney Arodin**

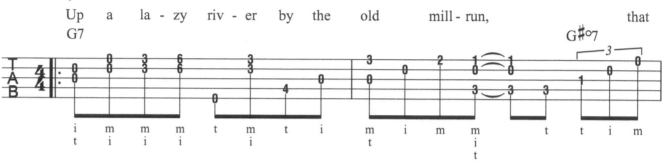

G tuning:
(5th-1st) G-D-G-B-D

**Key of B♭**

**Verse**
**Slowly**

Up a la - zy riv - er by the old mill - run,　that

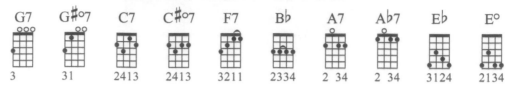

la - zy, la - zy riv - er in the noon - day sun,

lin - ger in the shade of a kind old tree;

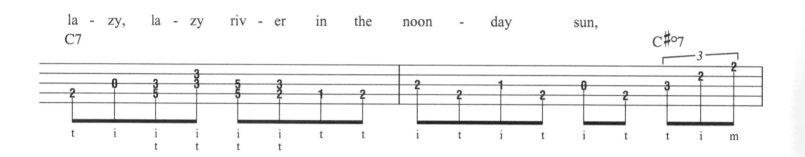

throw a - way your trou - bles, dream a dream with me.

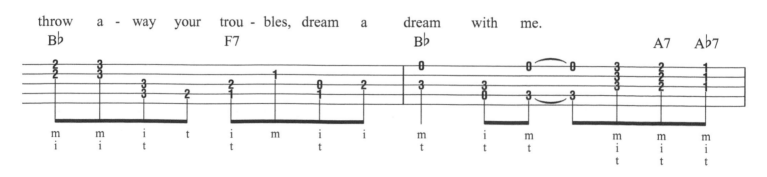

Up a la - zy riv - er, where the rob - in's song a -

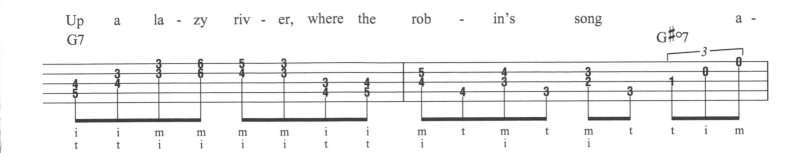

wakes a bright new morn - ing, we can loaf a - long.

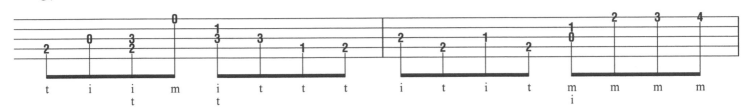

Blue skies up a - bove ev - 'ry - one's in love.

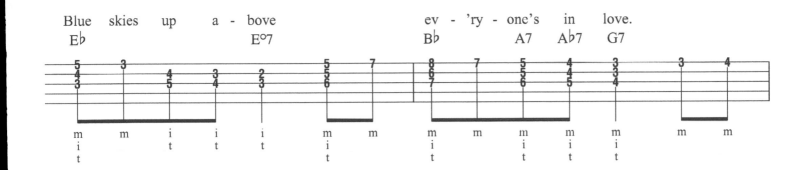

Up a la - zy riv - er, how hap - py you can be,

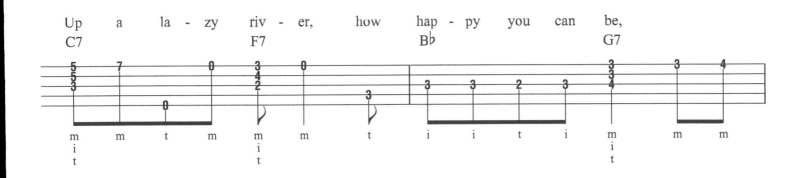

up a la - zy riv - er with me. me.

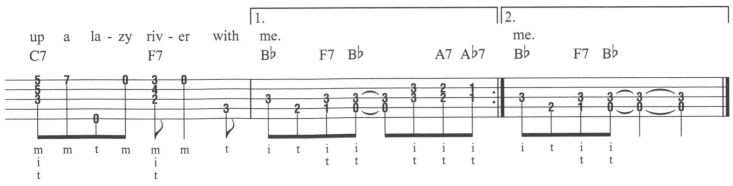

# Let the Rest of the World Go By

**Words by J. Keirn Brennan**
**Music by Ernest R. Ball**

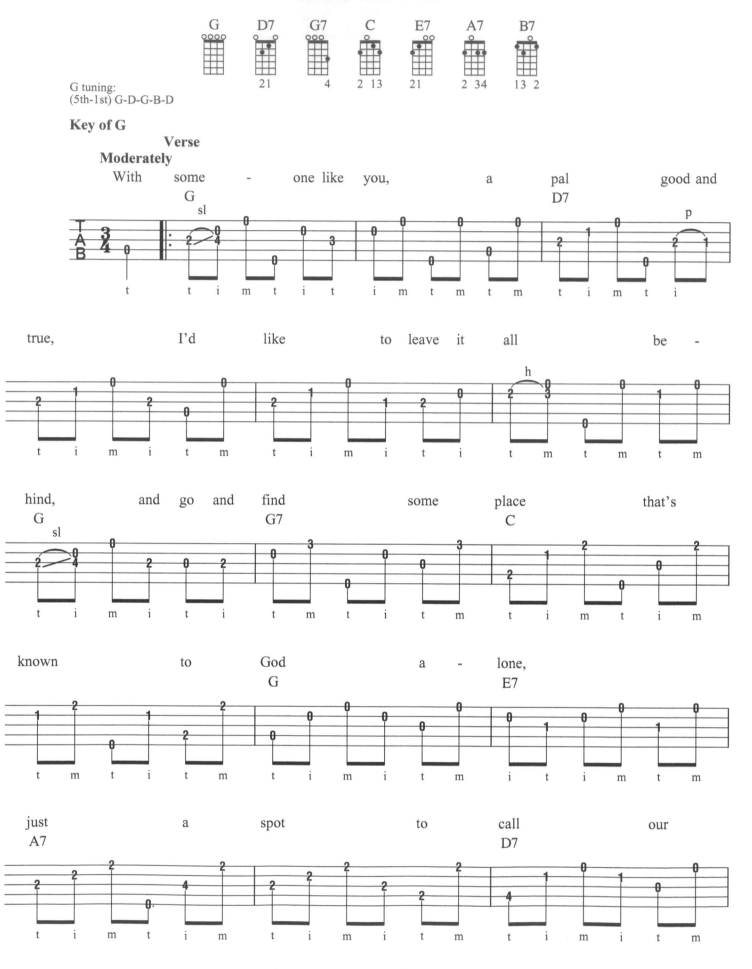

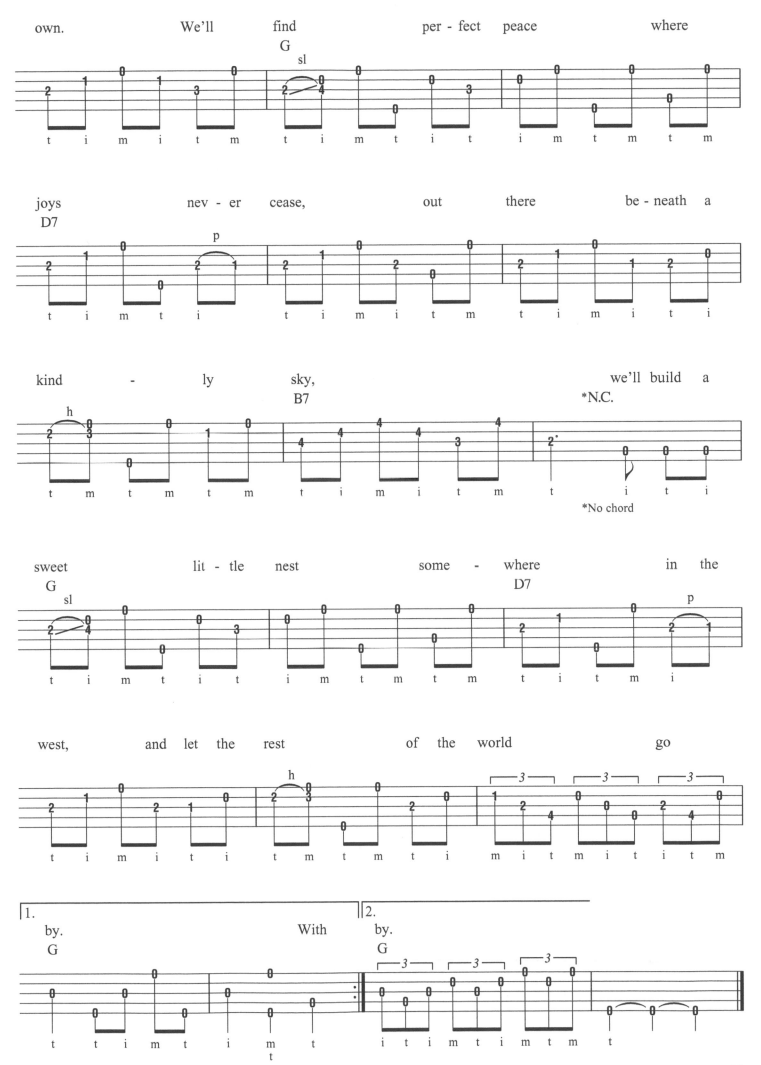

# Limehouse Blues

**from ZIEGFELD FOLLIES**

**Words by Douglas Furber**
**Music by Philip Braham**

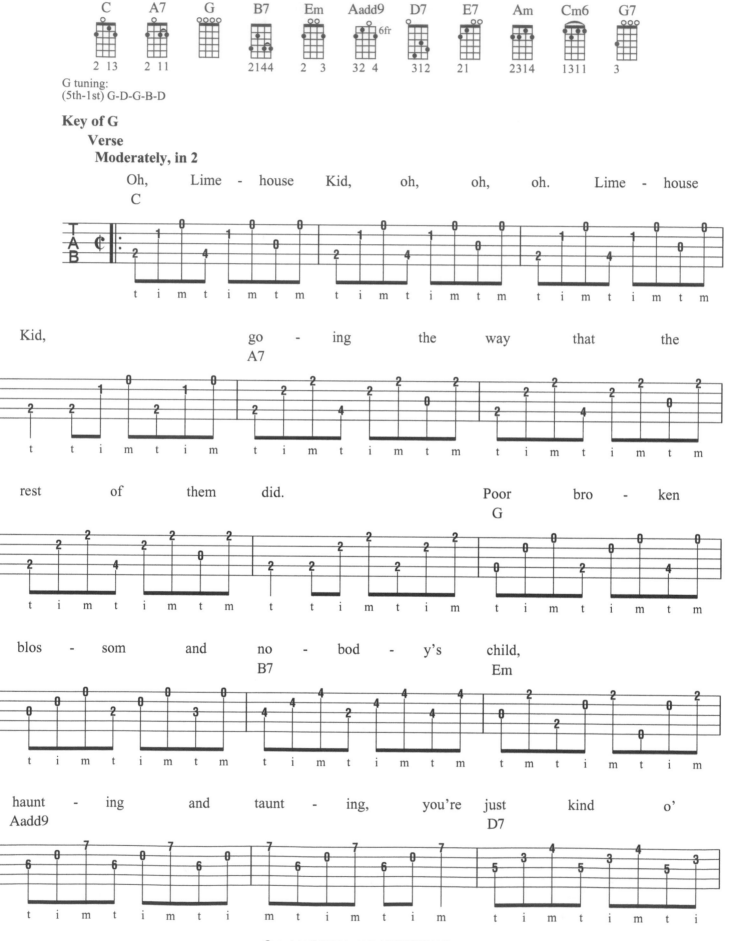

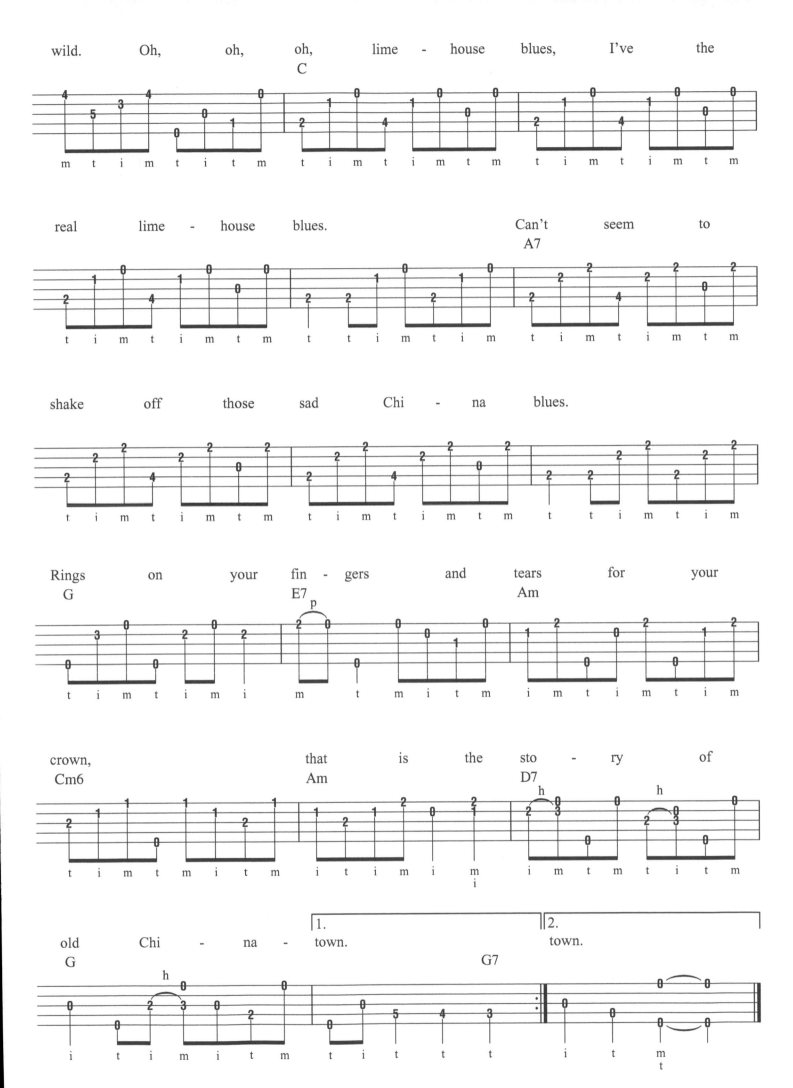

# Little Rock Getaway

**Music by Joe Sullivan**
**Words by Carl Sigman**

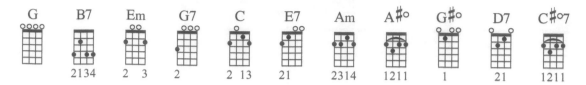

*G tuning:*
*(5th-1st) G-D-G-B-D*

**Key of G**

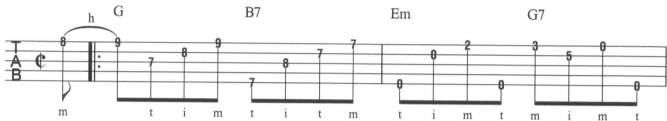

**A**

**Moderately, in 2**

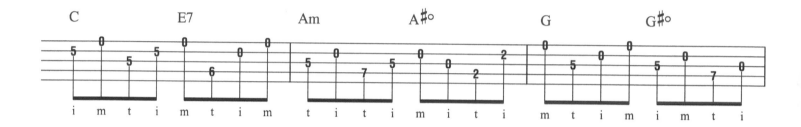

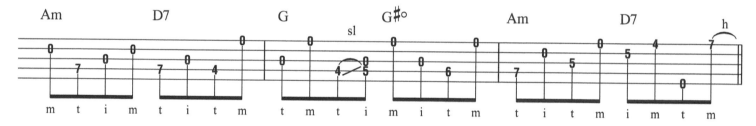

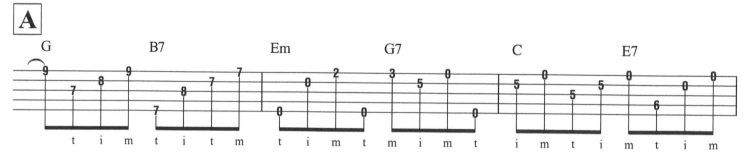

**A**

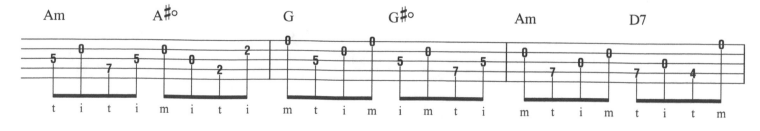

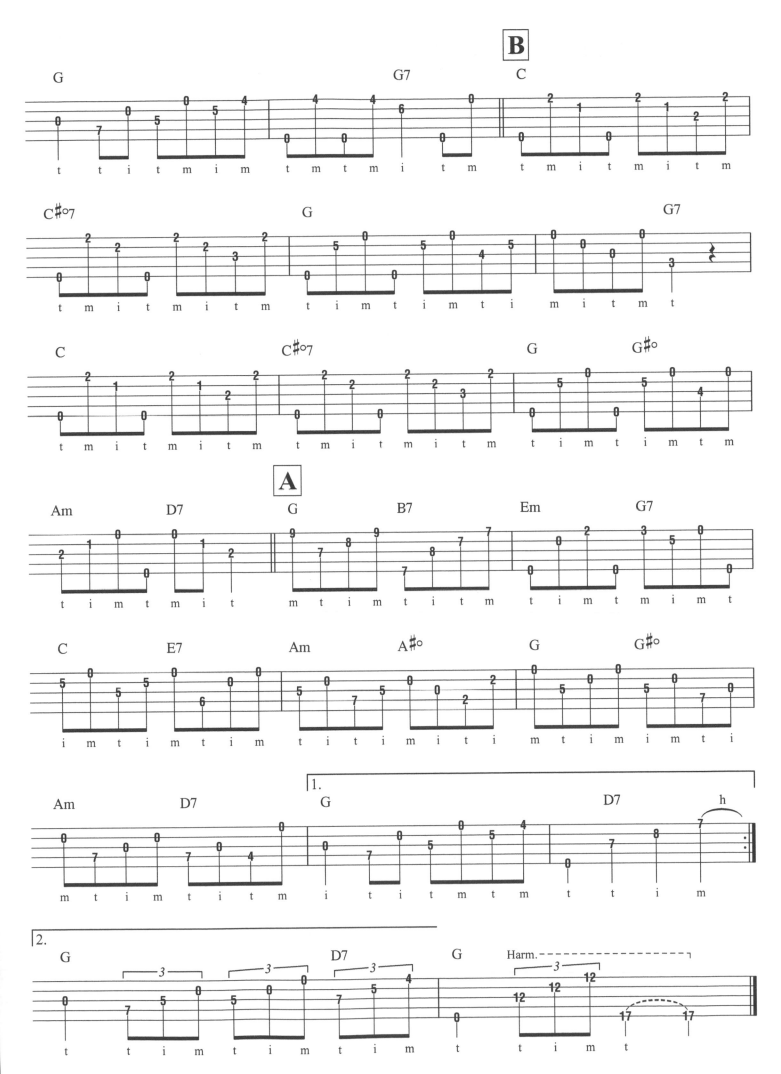

# Loveliest Night of the Year

**Lyric by Paul Francis Webster**
**Music by Irving Aaronson**

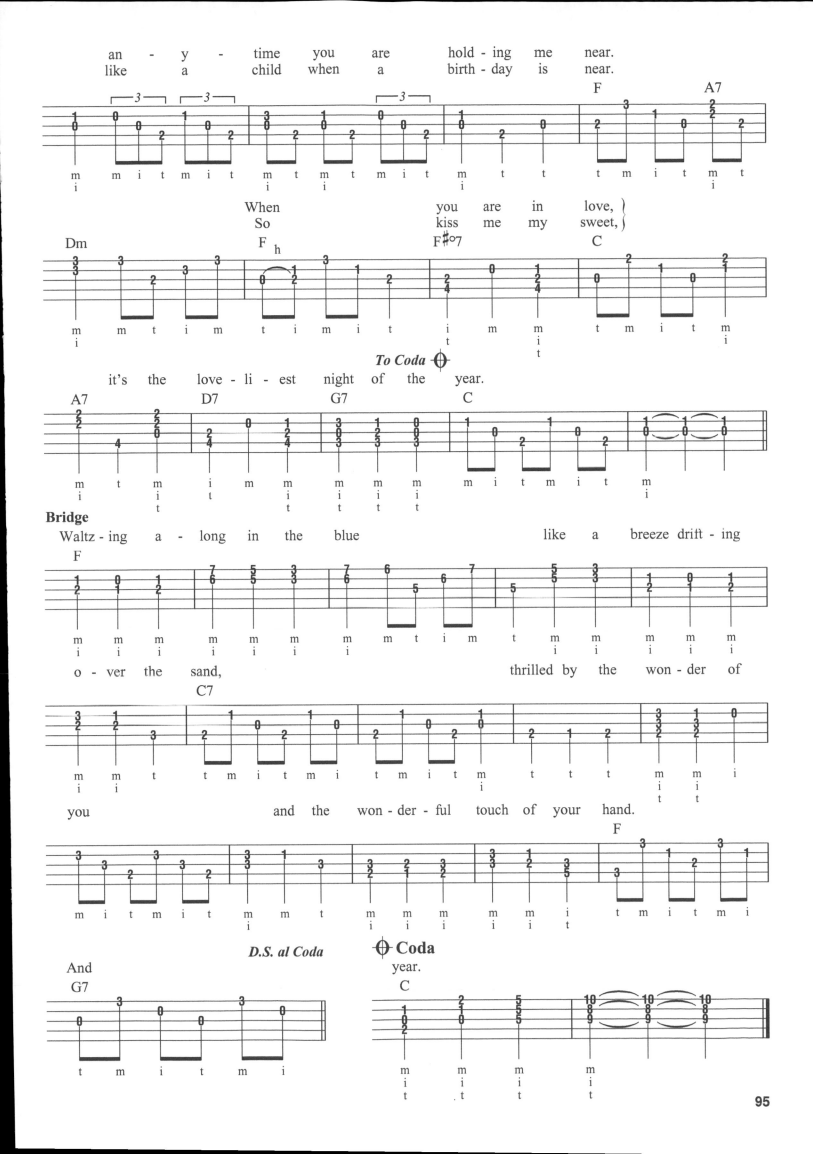

# Marie

### from the Motion Picture THE AWAKENING
### Words and Music by Irving Berlin

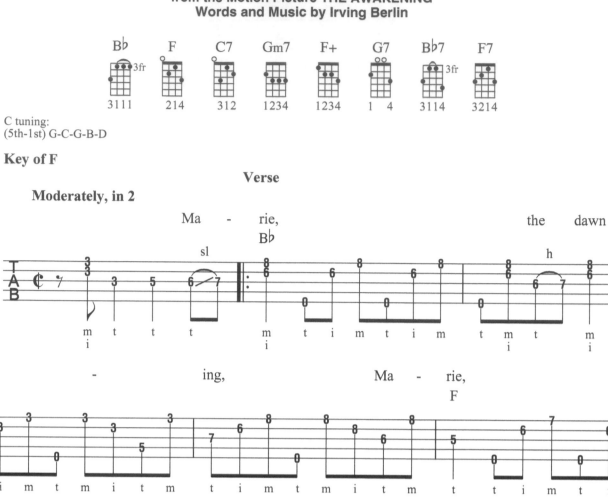

C tuning:
(5th-1st) G-C-G-B-D

**Key of F**

**Verse**

**Moderately, in 2**

Ma - rie,      the dawn is

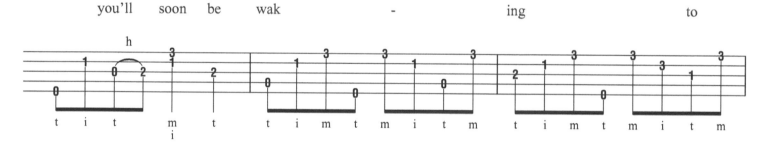

break - ing,    Ma - rie,

you'll soon be wak - ing    to

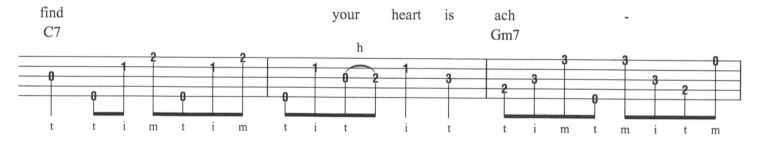

find    your heart is ach -
C7         Gm7

ing      and tears      will fall      as
C7         F          C7

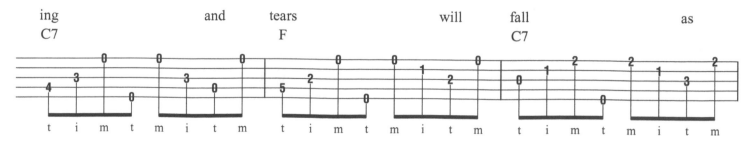

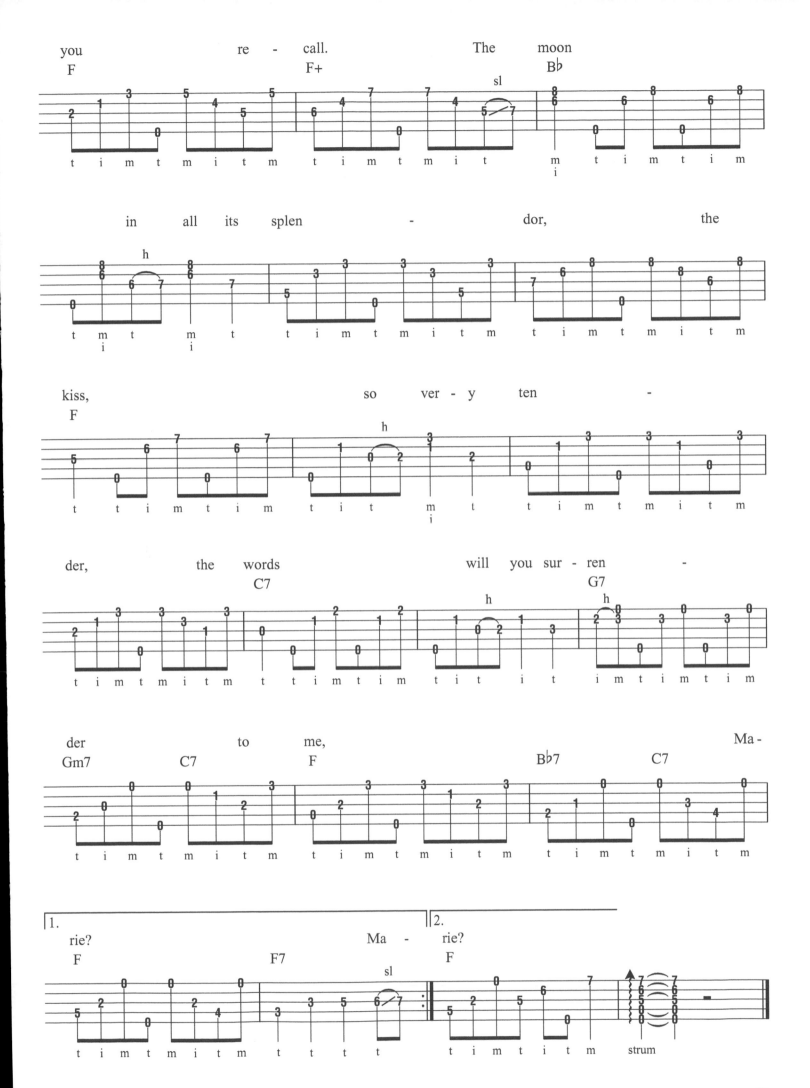

# Mexicali Rose

from MEXICALI ROSE
**Words by Helen Stone**
**Music by Jack B. Tenney**

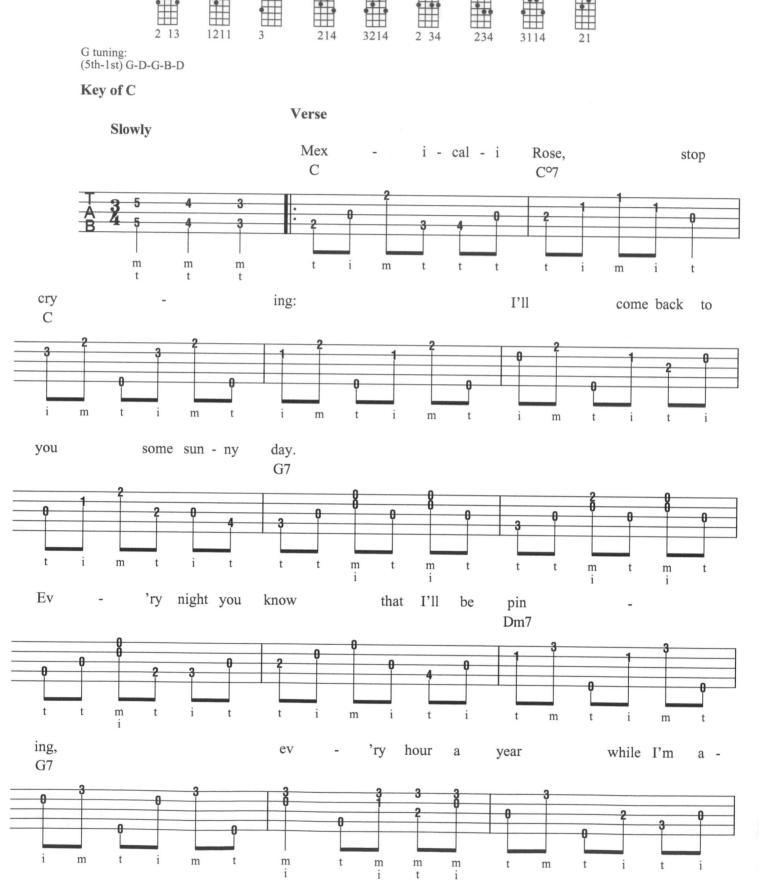

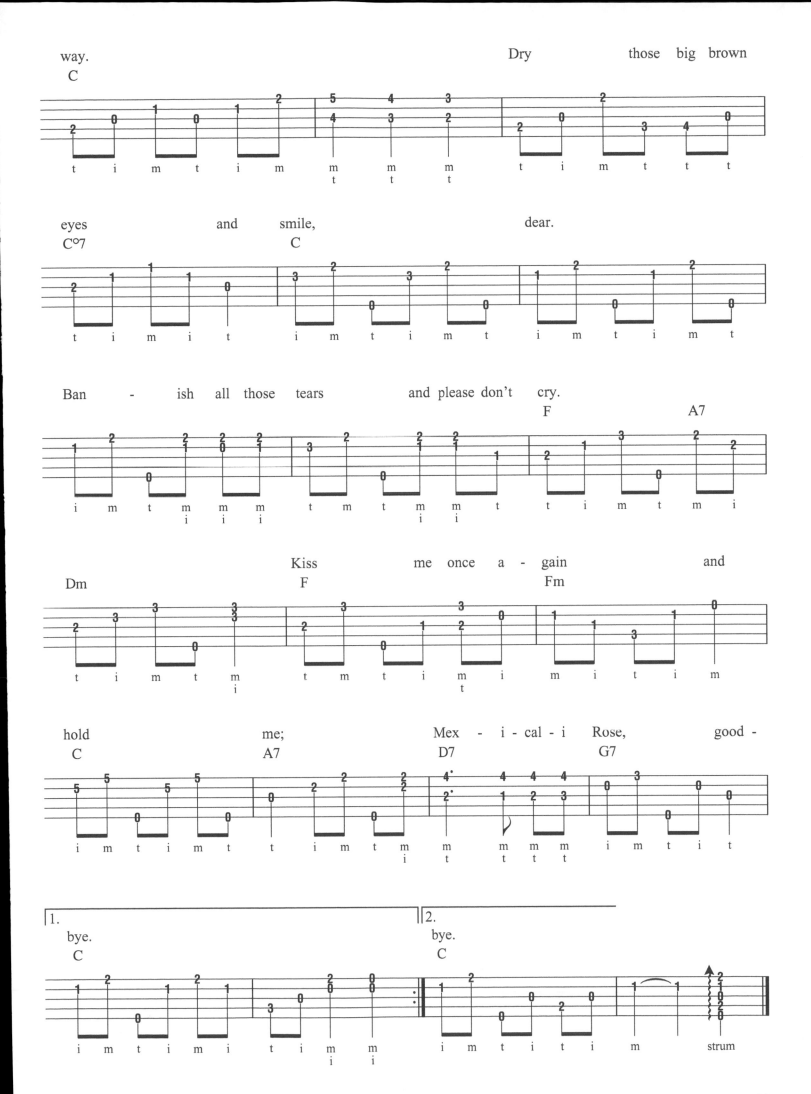

# Moonglow

**Words and Music by Will Hudson, Eddie De Lange and Irving Mills**

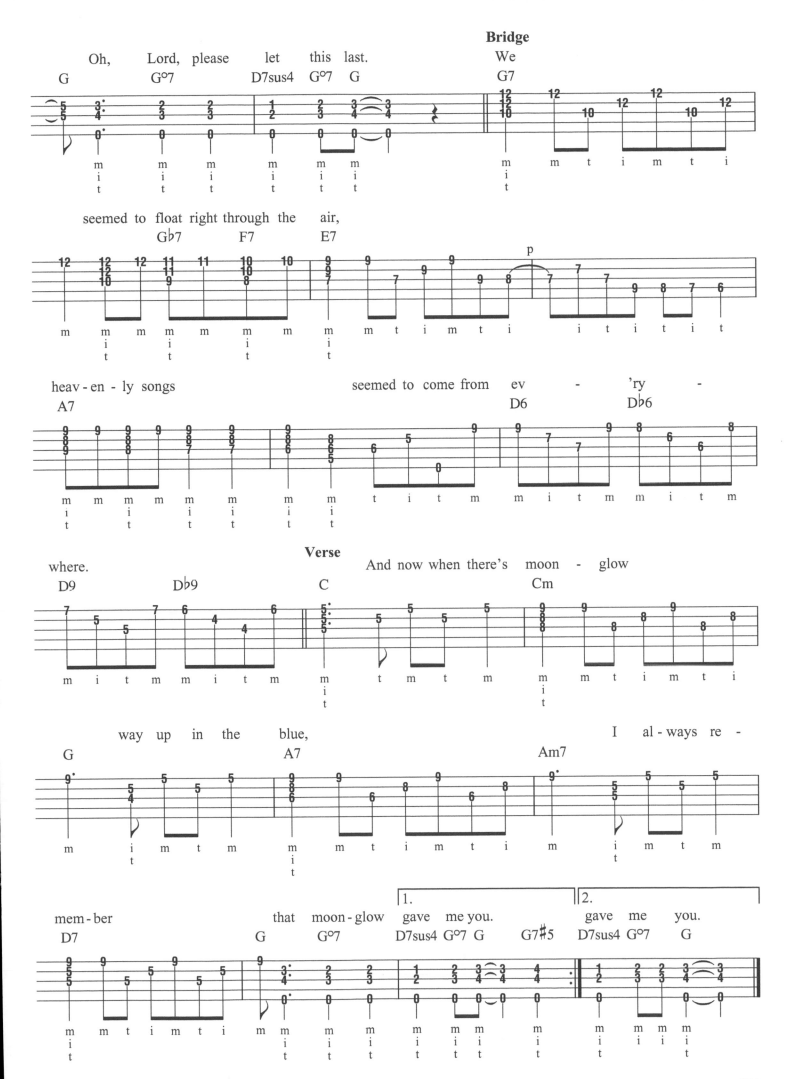

# Moonlight Bay

**Words by Edward Madden**
**Music by Percy Wenrich**

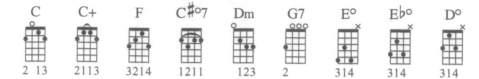

G tuning:
(5th-1st) G-D-G-B-D

**Key of C**

**Moderately**

**Verse**

We were sail - ing a - long

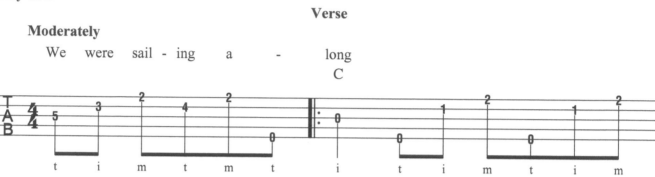

on     Moon - light     Bay.

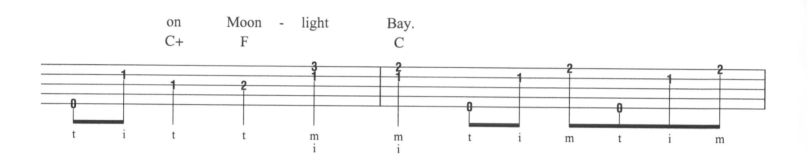

We could hear the voic - es ring - ing,

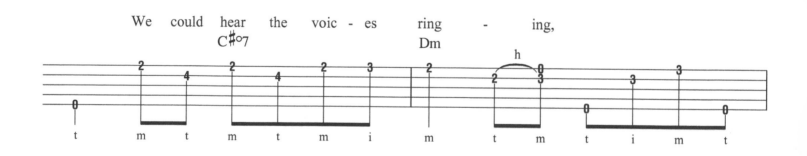

they     seemed     to     say:

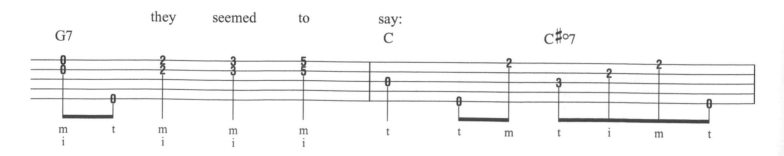

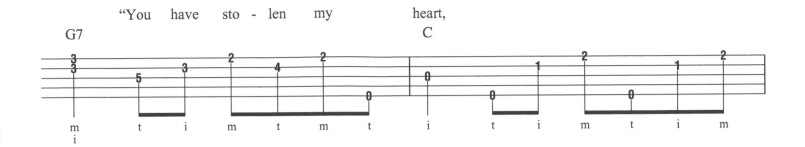

"You have sto - len my heart,

now don't go 'way!"

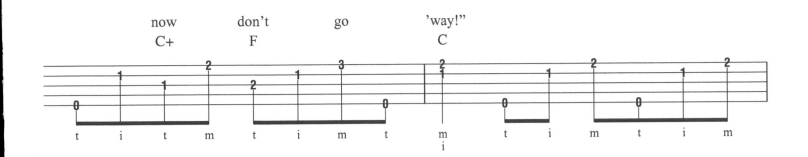

As we sang "Loves Old Sweet Song" on Moon - light

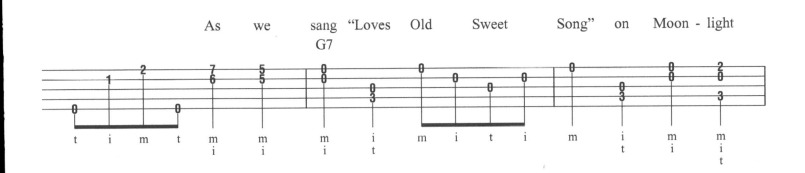

1.
Bay.

We were sail - ing a -

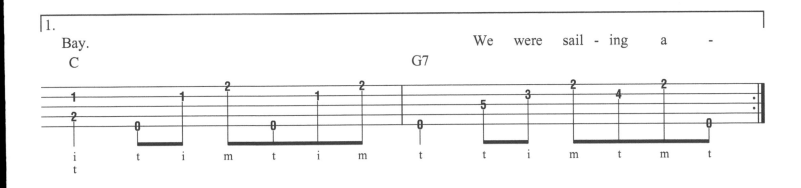

2.
Bay.

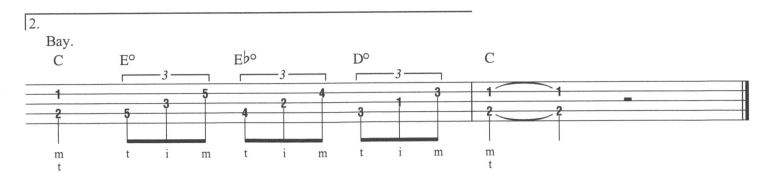

# My Blue Heaven

**Lyric by George Whiting**
**Music by Walter Donaldson**

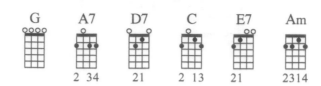

G tuning:
(5th-1st) G-D-G-B-D

**Key of G**

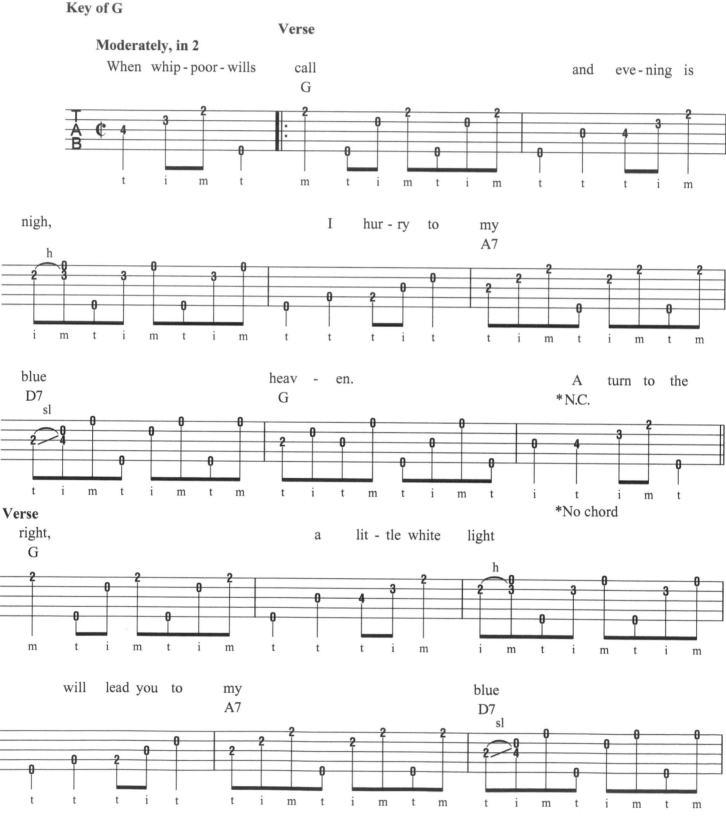

# My Dreams Are Getting Better All the Time

**Words by Mann Curtis**
**Music by Vic Mizzy**

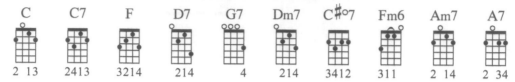

G tuning:
(5th-1st) G-D-G-B-D

**Key of C**

**Verse**

Slowly

Well,    what do you know, he smiled at    me in my dreams    last    night.    My

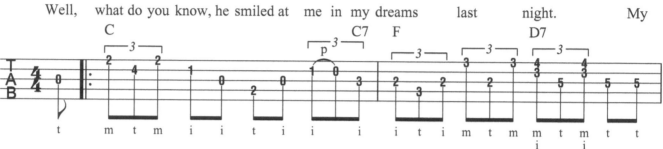

dreams    are get - ting bet - ter all    the    time.    And

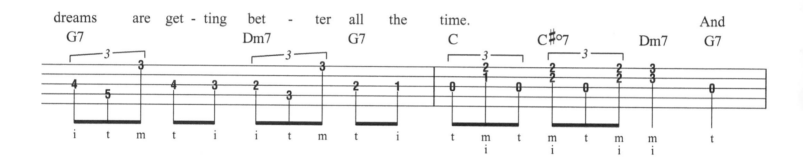

what do you know, he looked at    me in a    dif - f'rent    light.    My

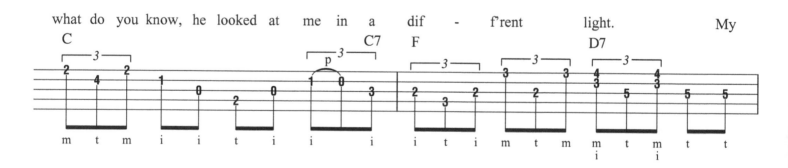

dreams    are get - ting bet - ter all    the    time.    To

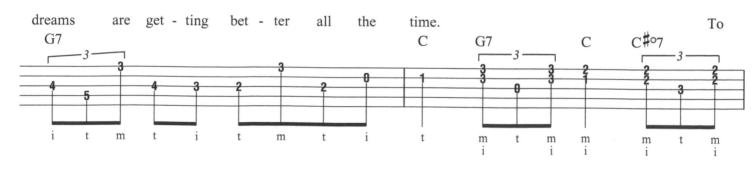

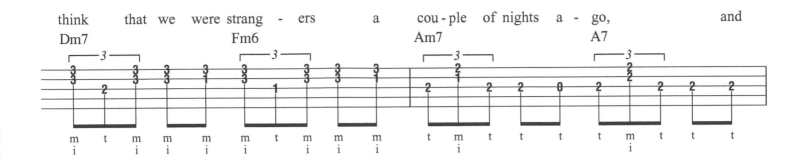

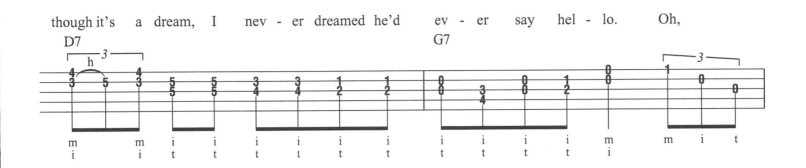

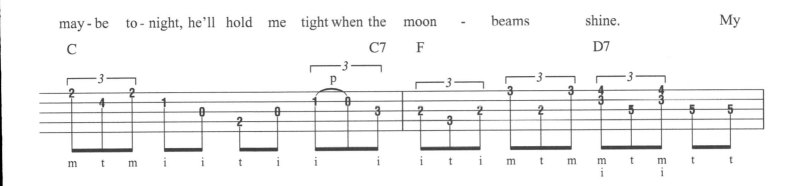

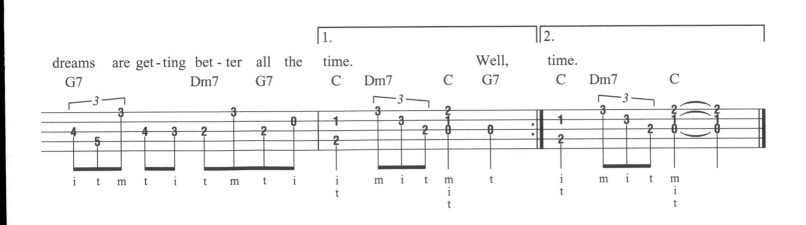

# Near You

**Words by Kermit Goell**
**Music by Francis Craig**

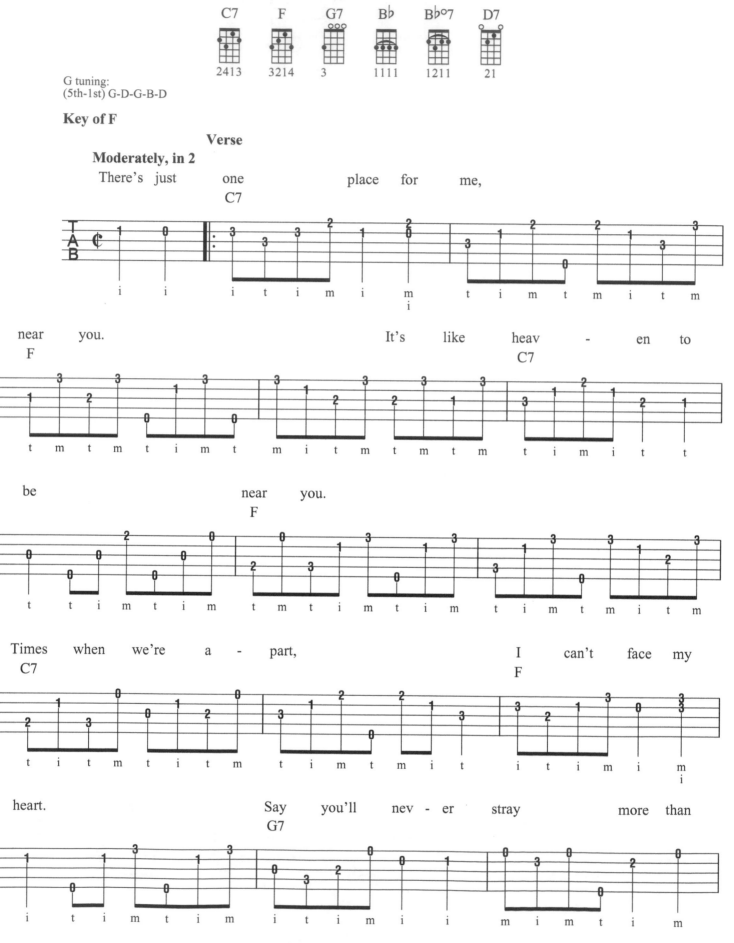

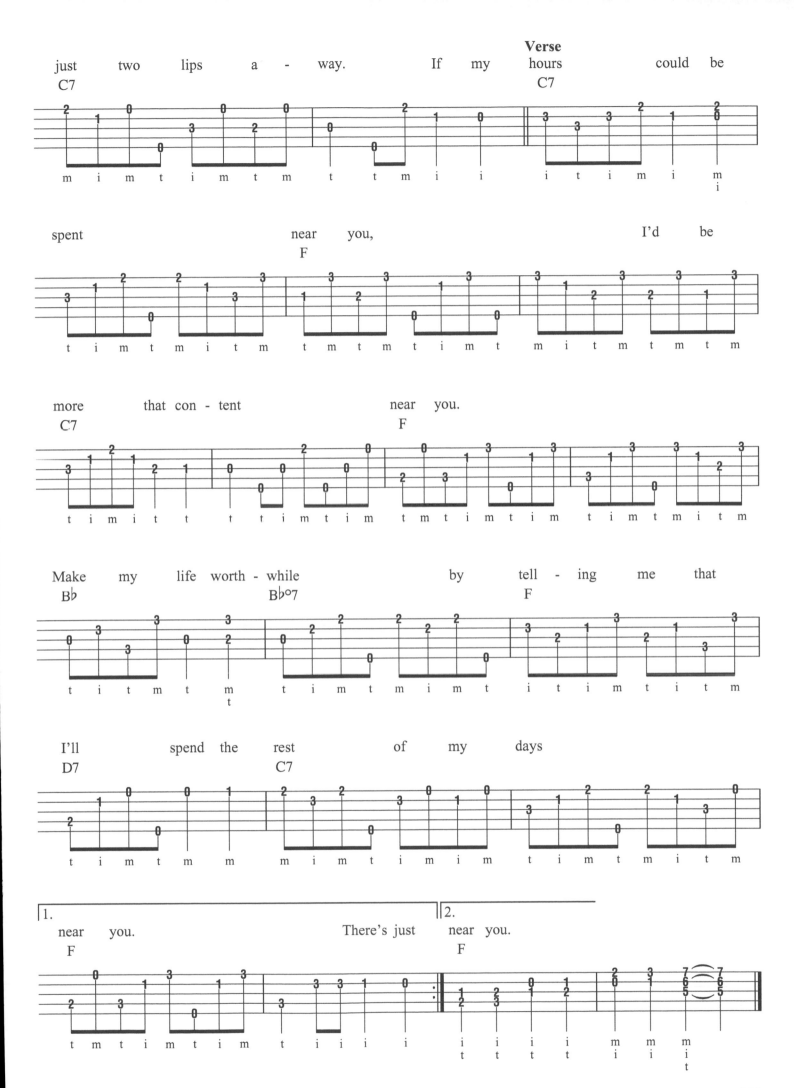

# The Nearness of You

from the Paramount Picture ROMANCE IN THE DARK

**Words by Ned Washington**
**Music by Hoagy Carmichael**

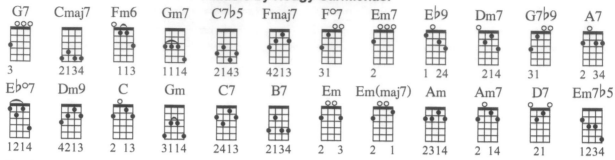

G tuning:
(5th-1st) G-D-G-B-D

**Key of C**

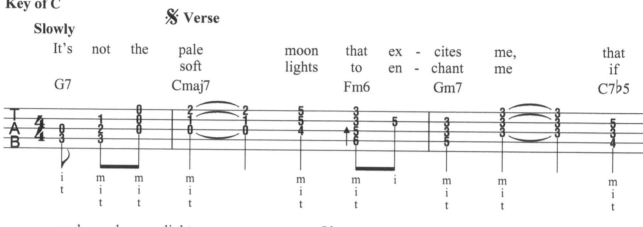

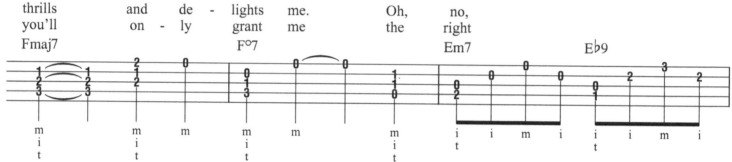

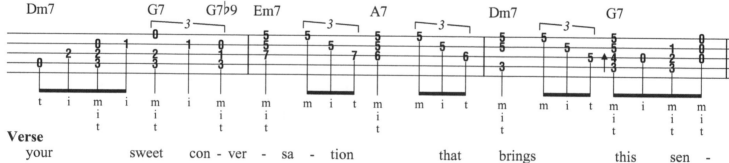

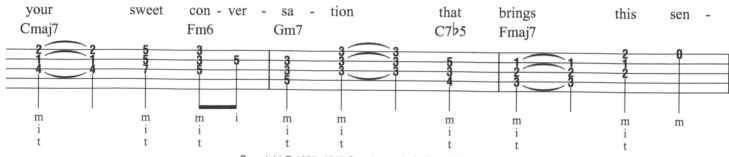

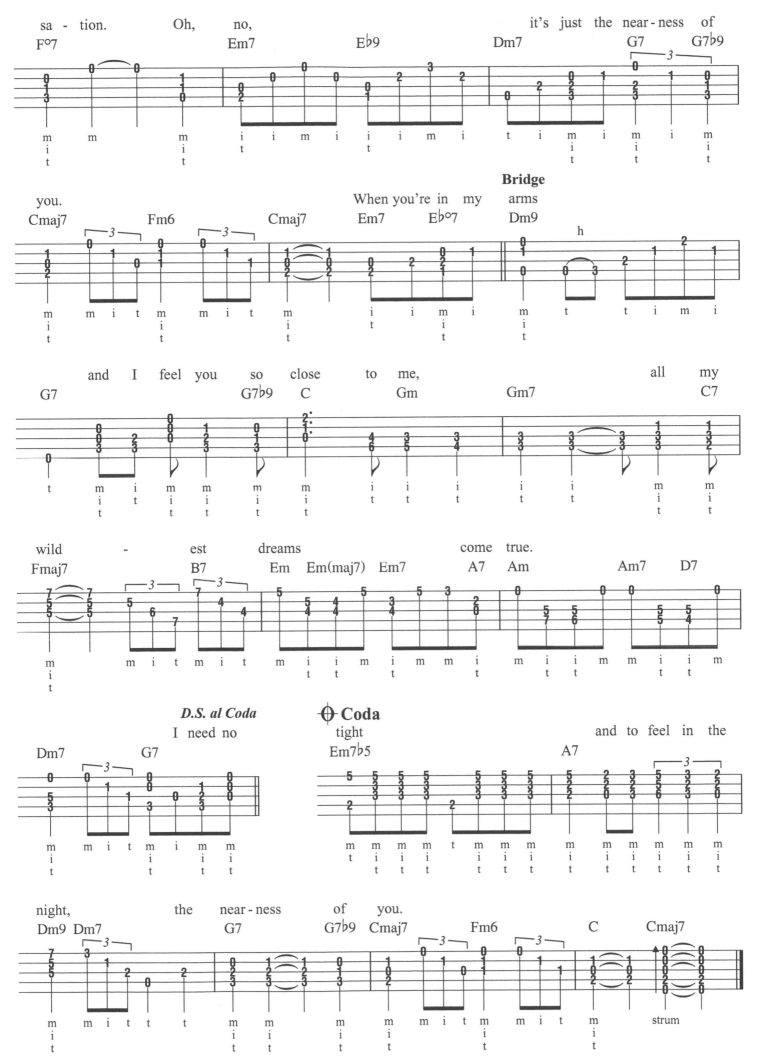

# Nice Work if You Can Get It

from A DAMSEL IN DISTRESS
Music and Lyrics by George Gershwin and Ira Gershwin

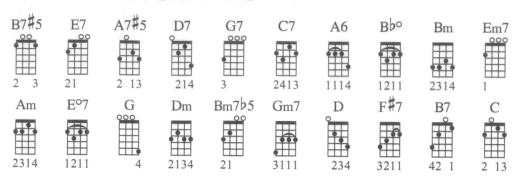

G tuning:
(5th-1st) G-D-G-B-D

**Key of G**

**Verse**
**Moderately**

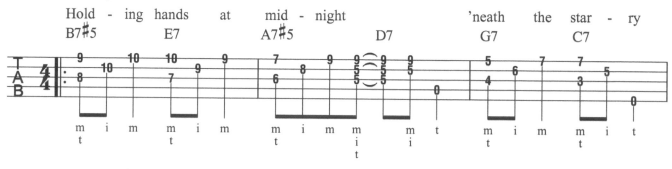

Hold - ing hands at mid - night 'neath the star - ry

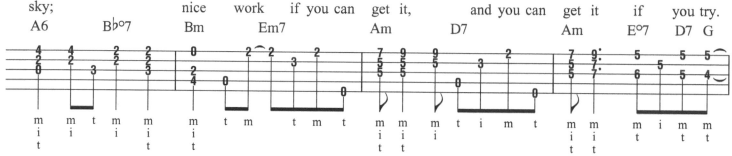

sky; nice work if you can get it, and you can get it if you try.

**Verse**

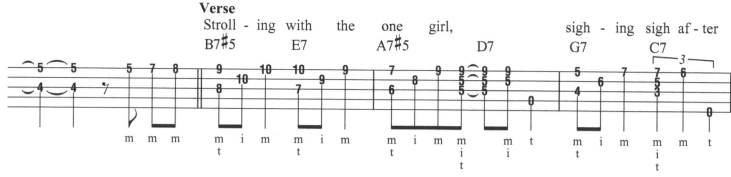

Stroll - ing with the one girl, sigh - ing sigh af - ter

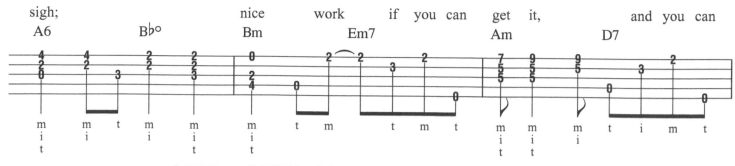

sigh; nice work if you can get it, and you can

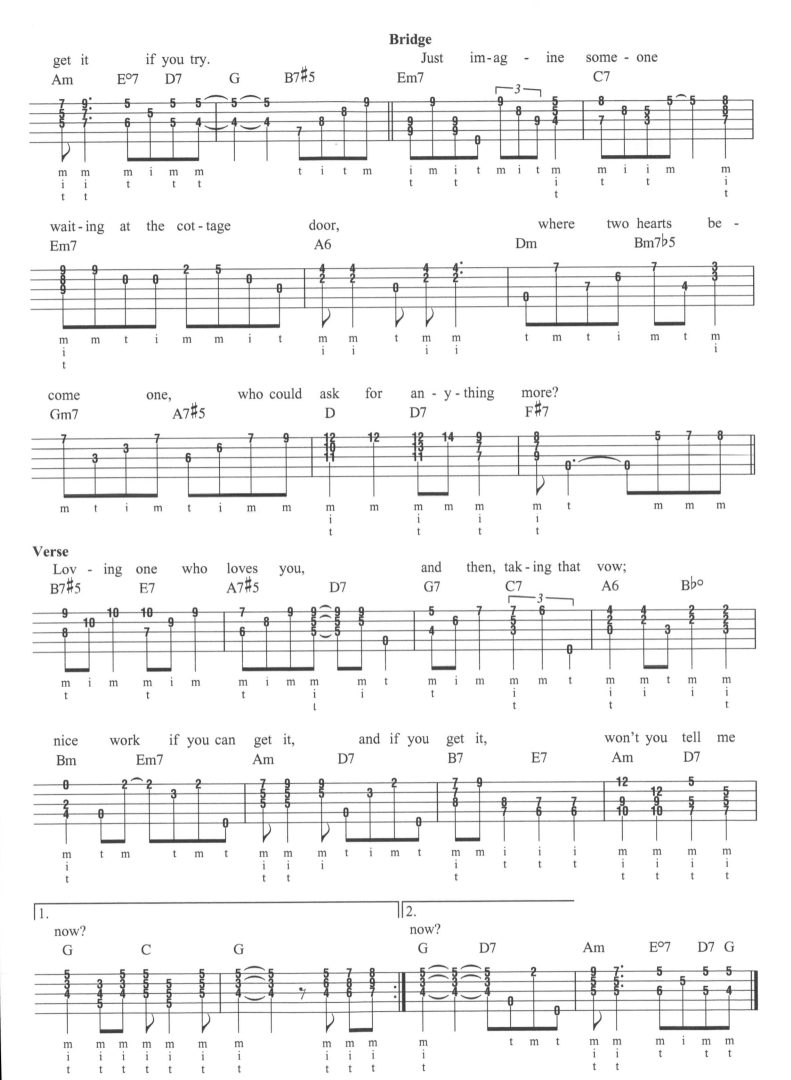

# Oh, Lady Be Good!

from LADY, BE GOOD!

**Music and Lyrics by George Gershwin and Ira Gershwin**

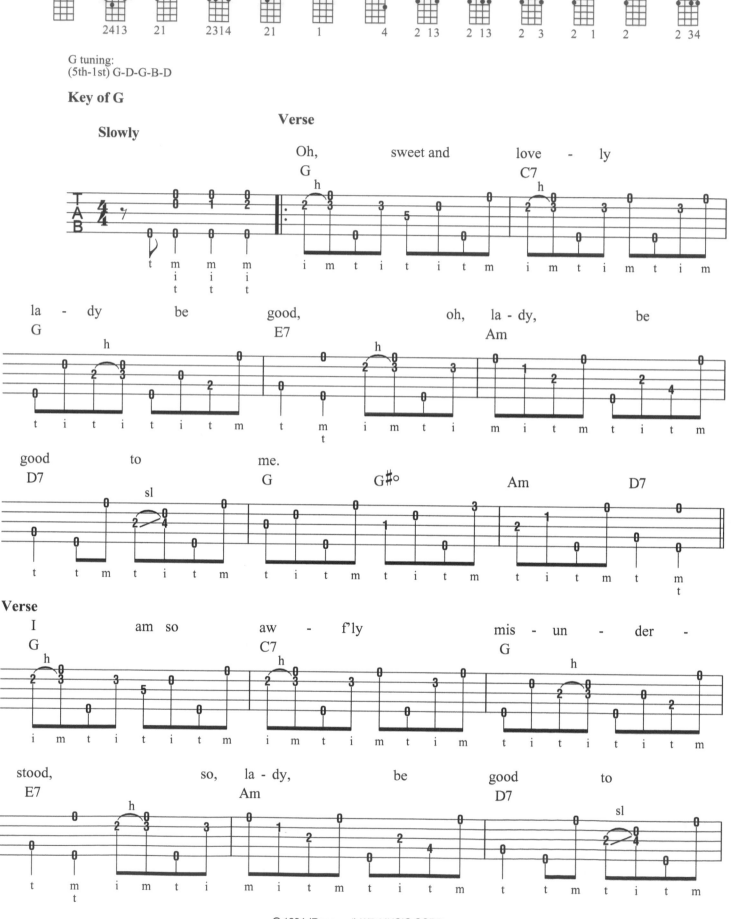

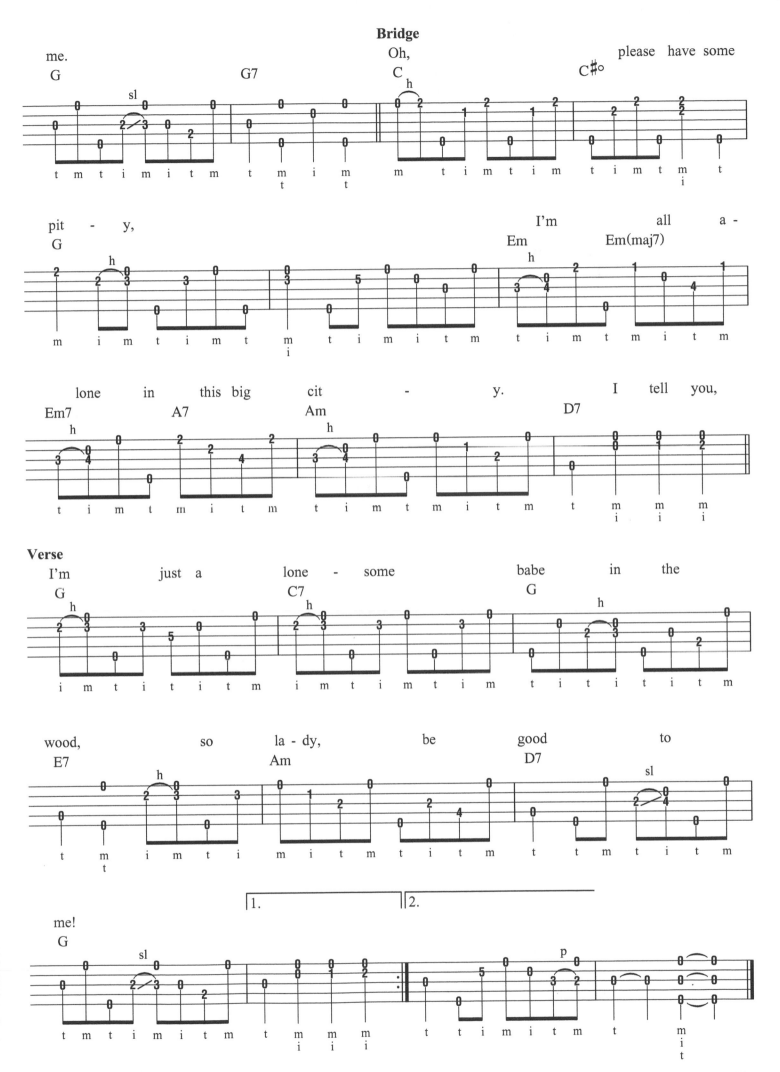

# Over the Rainbow

### from THE WIZARD OF OZ
**Music by Harold Arlen**
**Lyric by E.Y. "Yip" Harburg**

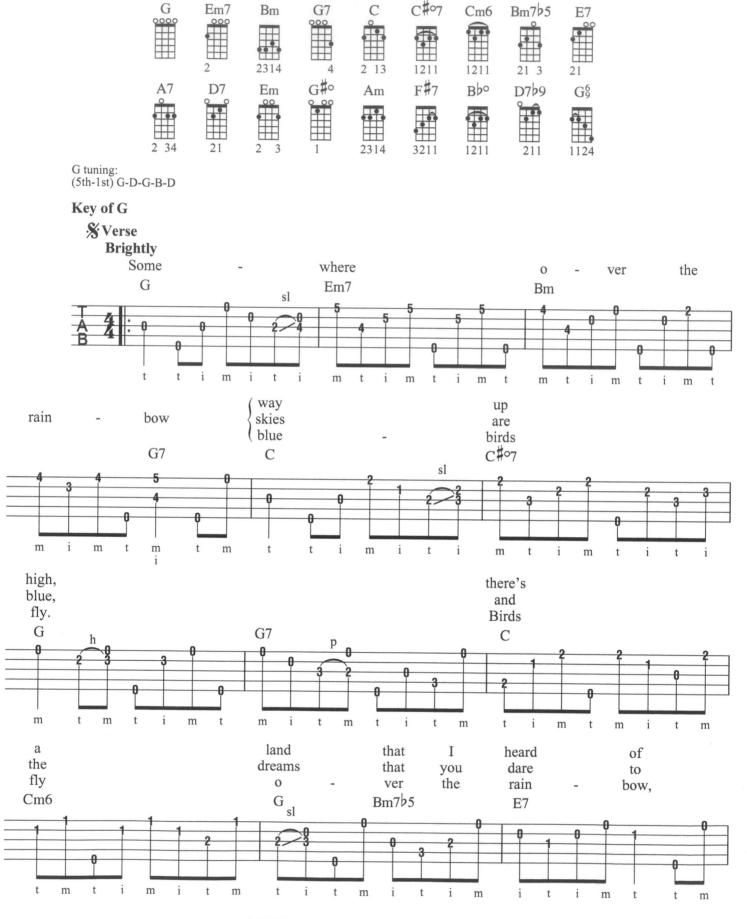

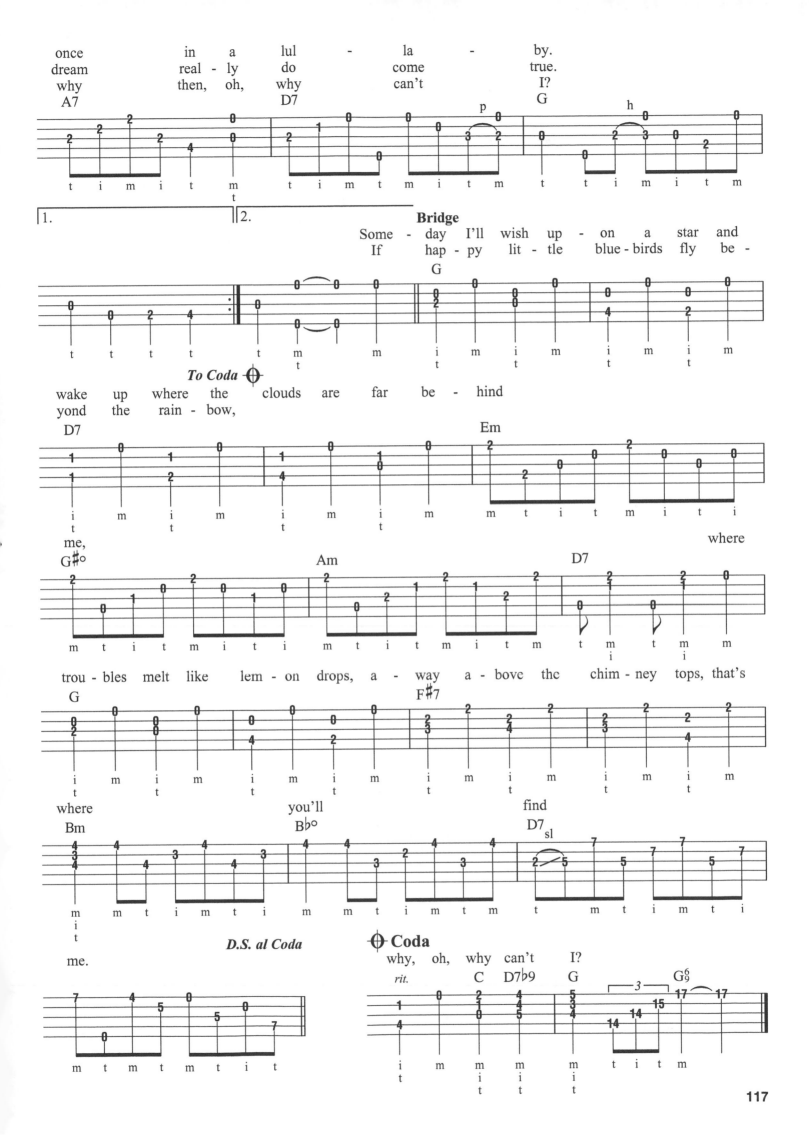

once    in  a  lul - la -    by.
dream    real - ly  do   come     true.
why    then, oh,  why   can't     I?

**Bridge**

Some - day I'll wish up - on a star and
If  hap - py lit - tle blue - birds fly be -

*To Coda*

wake up where the clouds are far be - hind
yond the rain - bow,

me,                   where

trou - bles melt like lem - on drops, a - way a - bove the chim - ney tops, that's

where      you'll         find

me.

*D.S. al Coda*    **Coda**

why, oh, why can't  I?

*rit.*

117

# Paper Doll

**Words and Music by Johnny S. Black**

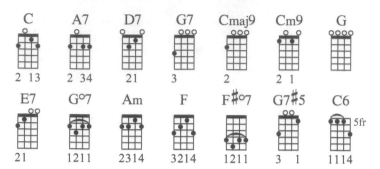

C    A7    D7    G7    Cmaj9    Cm9    G

2 13  2 34   21    3      2       2 1

E7    G°7    Am    F    F#°7    G7#5    C6

21    1211   2314  3214  1211    3  1    1114    5fr

G tuning:
(5th-1st) G-D-G-B-D

**Key of C**

Slowly ( ♫ = ♩♪ )

**Verse**

I'm goin' to buy a pa - per doll that I can
C                                          A7

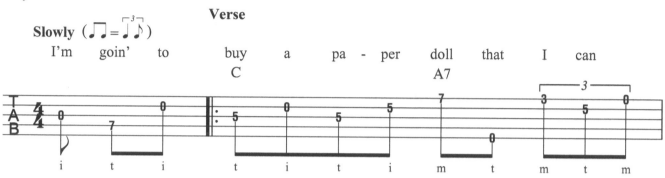

i    t    i        t    i    t    i    m    t    m    t    m

call    my    own,    a    doll    that    oth - er    fel - lows    can - not
D7                                    G7

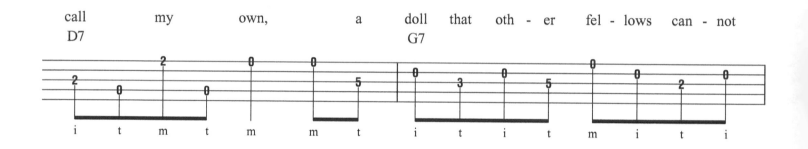

i    t    m    t    m    m    t    i    t    i    t    m    i    t    i

steal.    And    then    the    flir - ty,    flir - ty    guys    with    their
C                Cmaj9                    Cm9

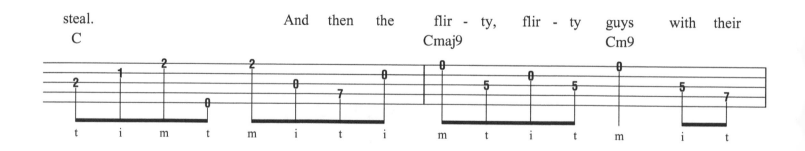

t    i    m    t    m    i    t    i    m    t    i    t    m    i    t

flir - ty,    flir - ty    eyes    will    have    to    flirt    with    dol - lies    that    are
G                E7                D7

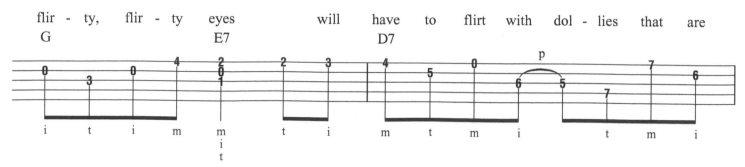

i    t    i    m    m    t    i    m    t    m    i    t    m    i
         m
         i
         t

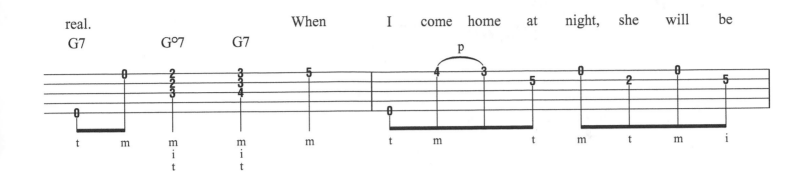

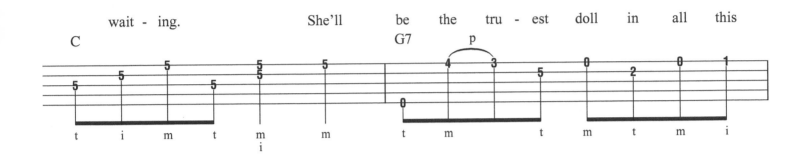

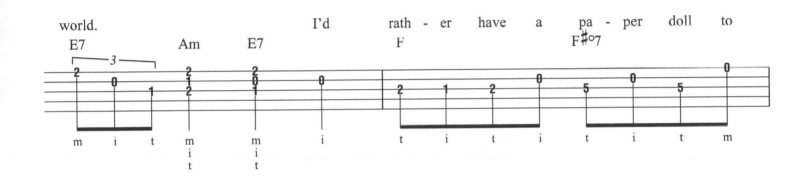

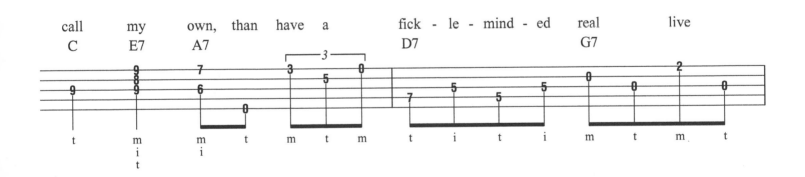

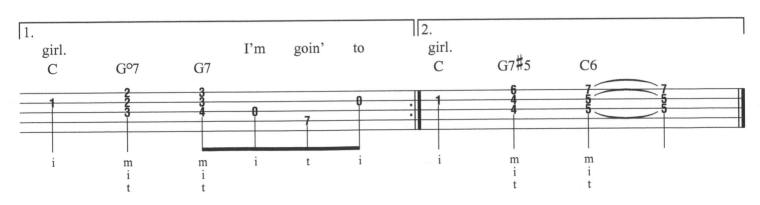

# Pennies from Heaven

from PENNIES FROM HEAVEN
Words by John Burke
Music by Arthur Johnston

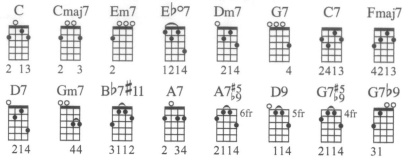

G tuning:
(5th-1st) G-D-G-B-D

**Key of C**
**Verse**
**Moderately**

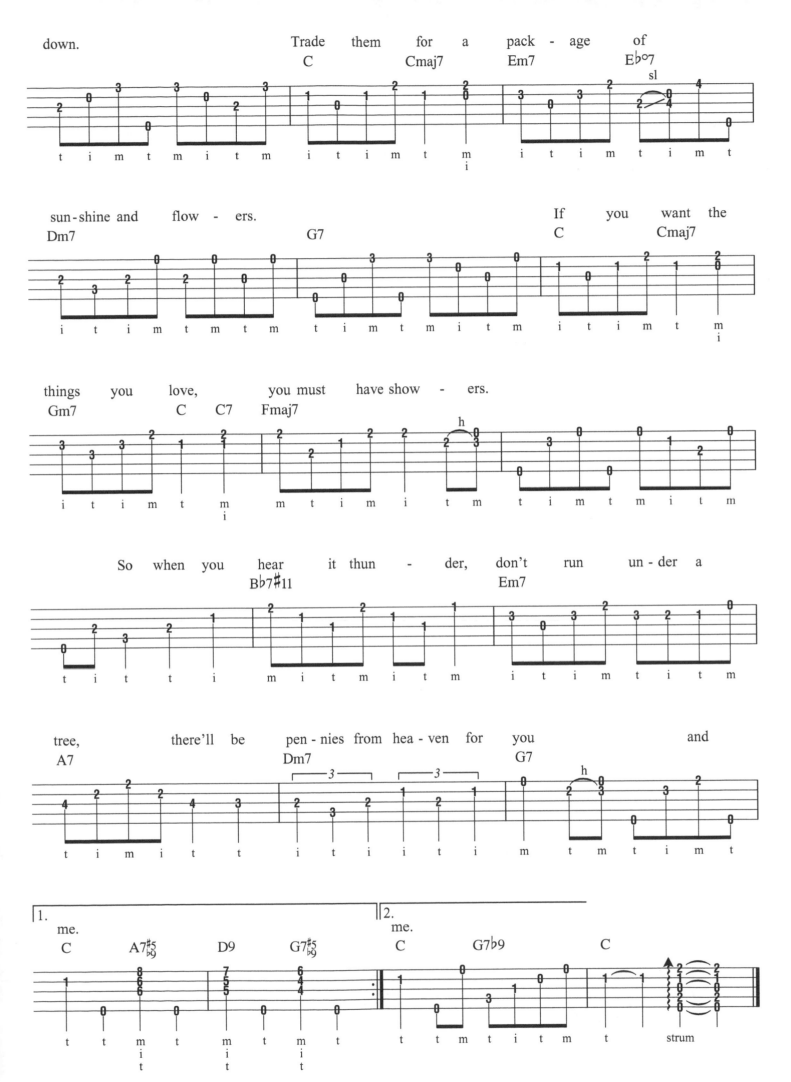

# Sioux City Sue

Words by Ray Freedman
Music by Dick Thomas

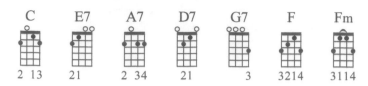

G tuning:
(5th-1st) G-D-G-B-D

**Key of C**

**Verse**
**Moderately, in 2**

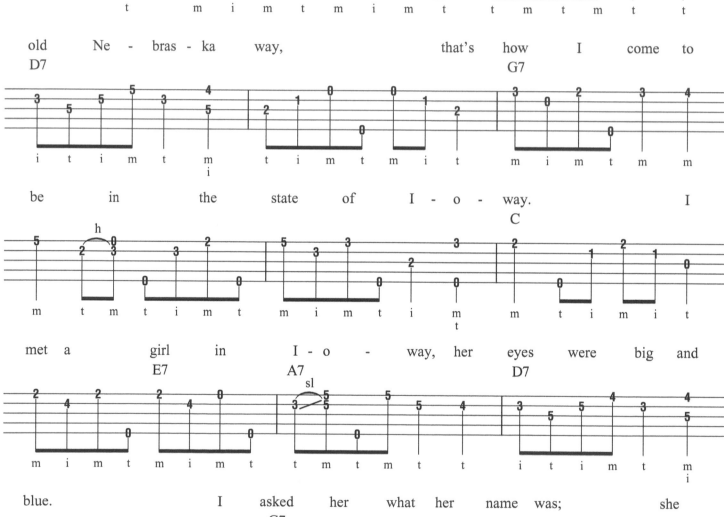

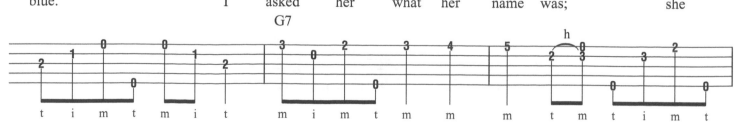

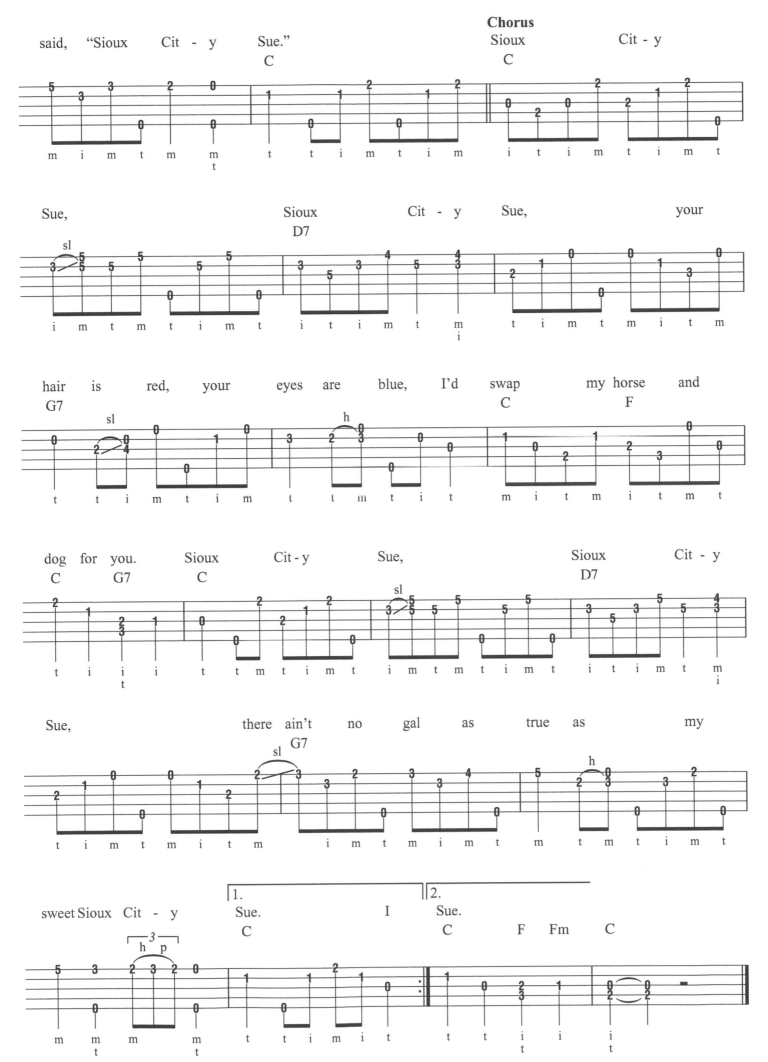

# Stardust

**Words by Mitchell Parish**
**Music by Hoagy Carmichael**

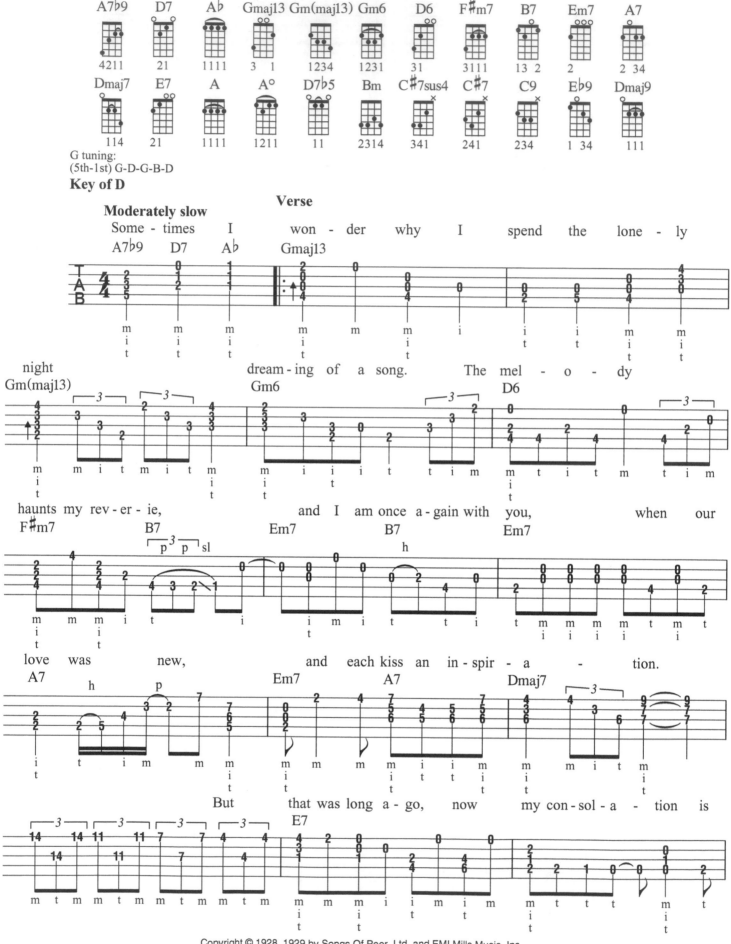

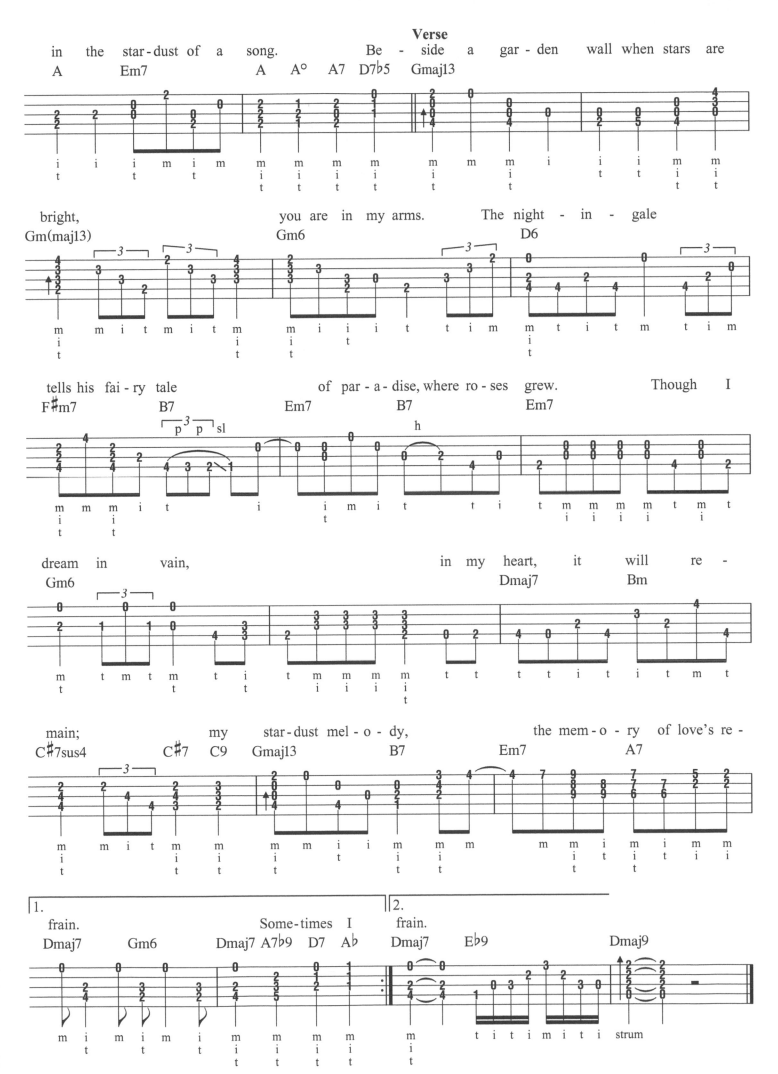

# Stumbling

**Words and Music by Zez Confrey**

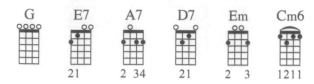

G tuning:
(5th-1st) G-D-G-B-D

**Key of G**

**Verse**
**Moderately, in 2**

Stum-bling all a - round, stum-bling all a - round, stum-bling all a -
G

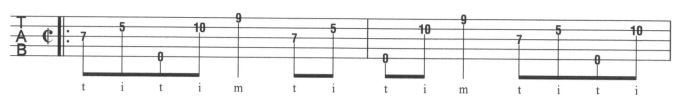

round so fun - ny. Stum-bling here and there, stum-bling
E7                  A7

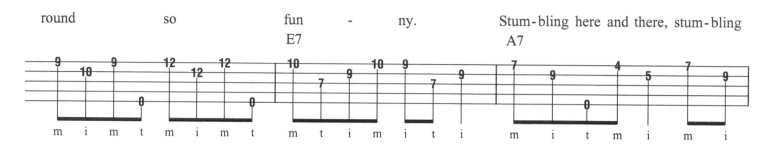

ev - 'ry-where, and I must de - clare:          I stepped right

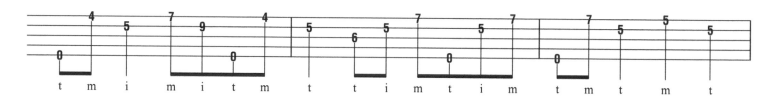

on her toes,      and when she bumped my nose,
D7                               Em

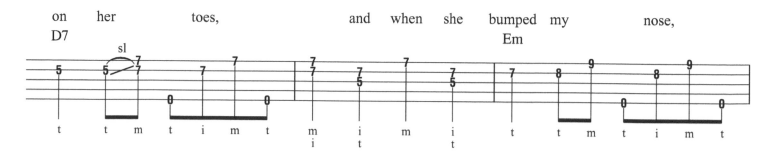

I fell and when I rose,      I felt a -
A7

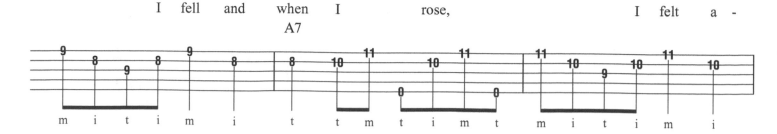

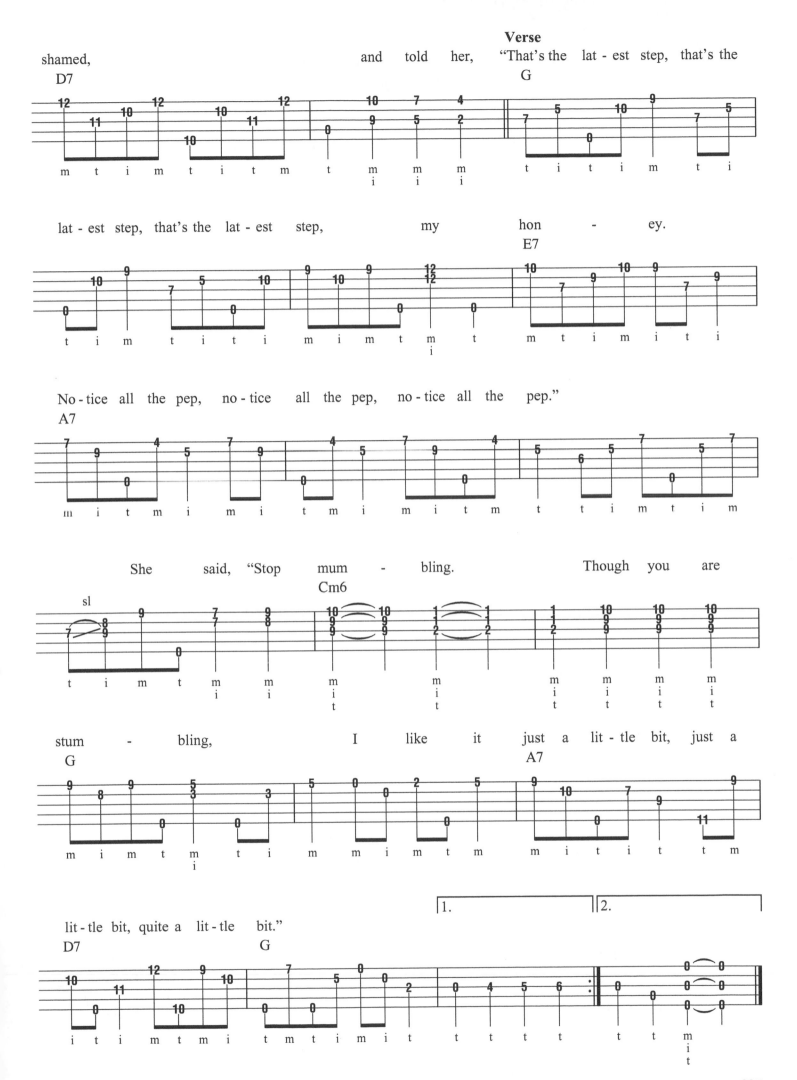

shamed,
D7

and told her, "That's the lat - est step, that's the
G

lat - est step, that's the lat - est step, my hon - ey.
E7

No - tice all the pep, no - tice all the pep, no - tice all the pep."
A7

She said, "Stop mum - bling.
Cm6

Though you are

stum - bling,
G

I like it just a lit - tle bit, just a
A7

lit - tle bit, quite a lit - tle bit."
D7                    G

1.                    2.

# Sweet Georgia Brown

**Words and Music by Ben Bernie, Maceo Pinkard and Kenneth Casey**

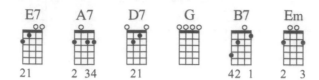

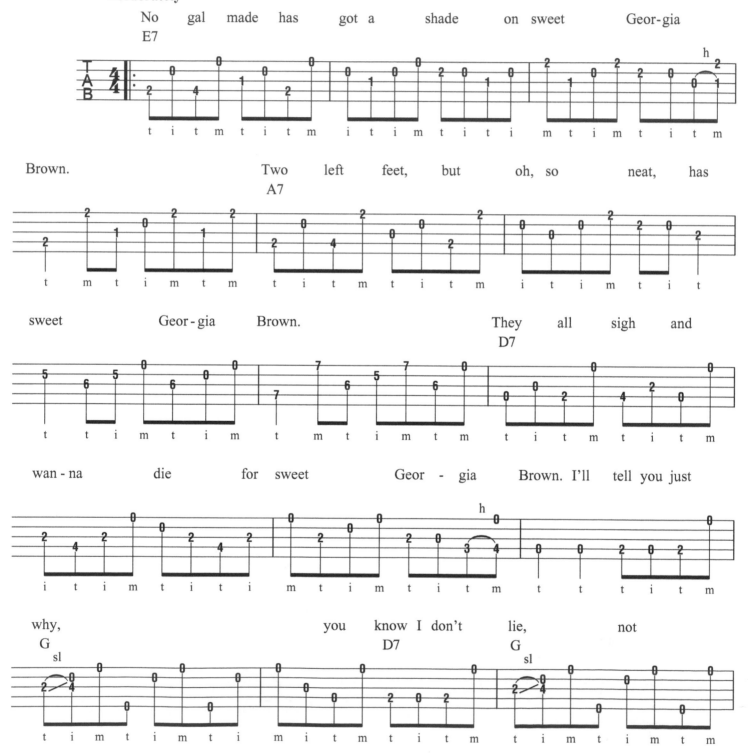

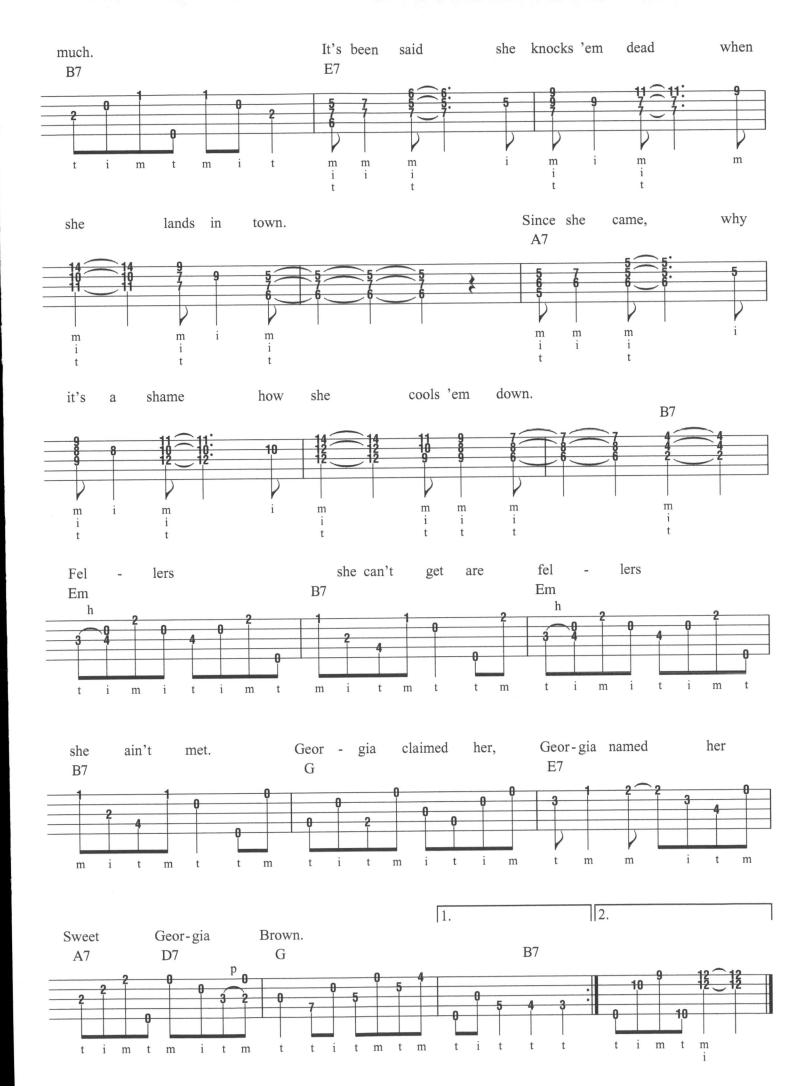

# Sweet Sue–Just You

from RHYTHM PARADE
Words by Will J. Harris
Music by Victor Young

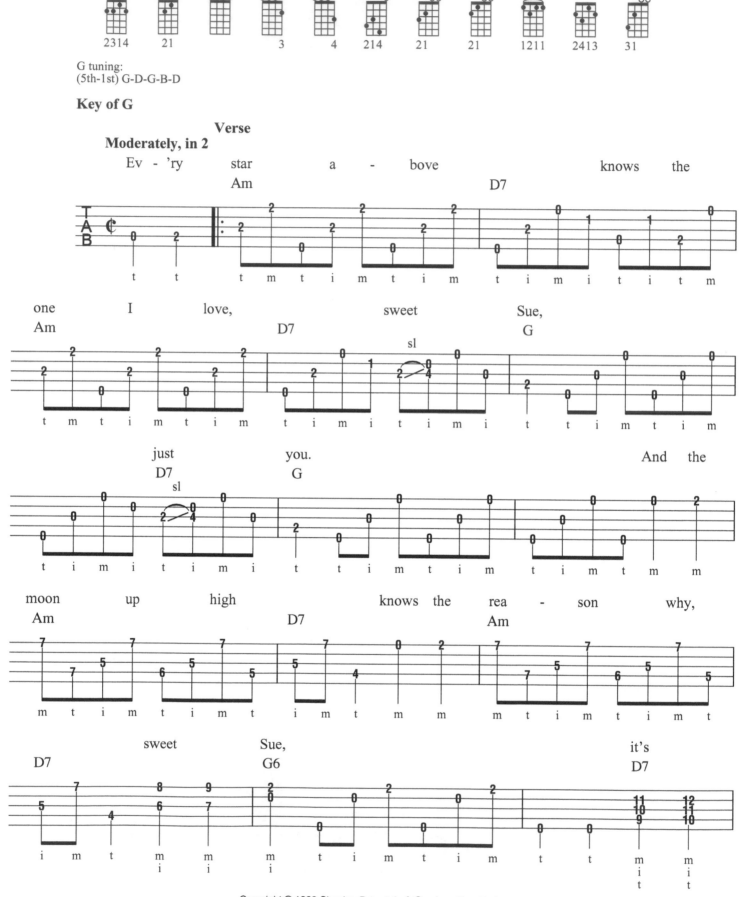

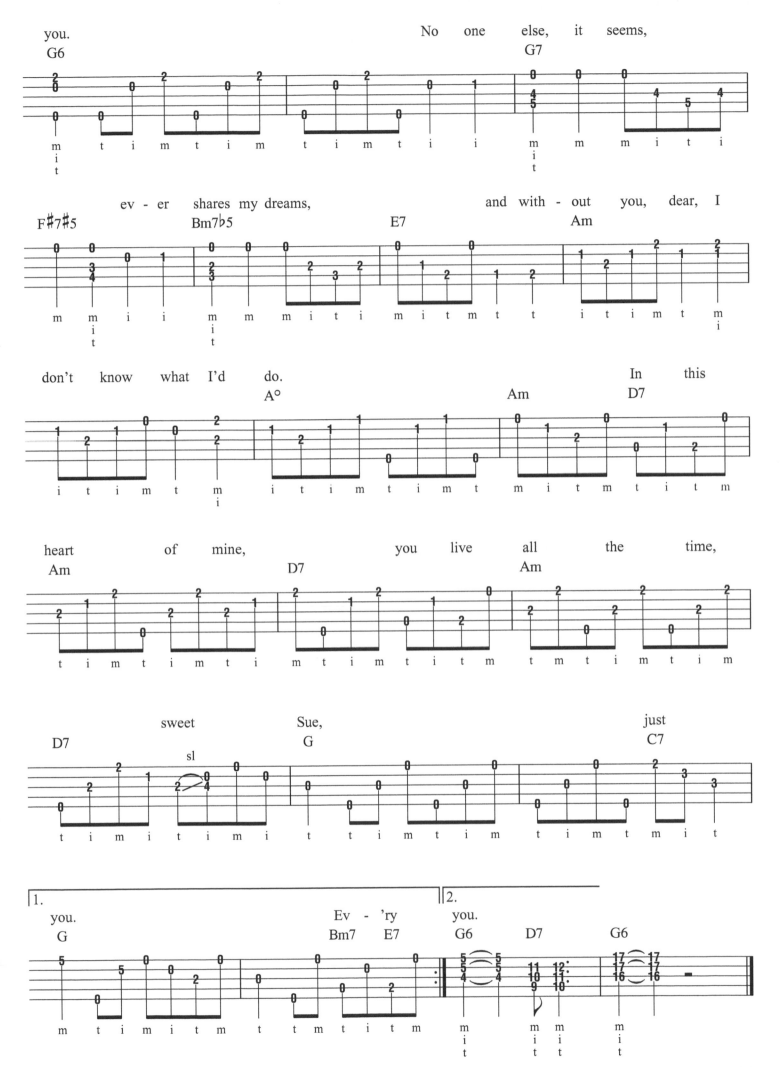

# Swinging on a Star

from GOING MY WAY
**Words by Johnny Burke**
**Music by Jimmy Van Heusen**

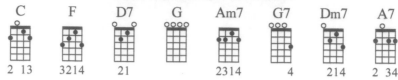

G tuning:
(5th-1st) G-D-G-B-D

**Key of C**

**Verse**
**Moderately, in 2**

# Take Me Out to the Ball Game

**Words by Jack Norworth**
**Music by Albert von Tilzer**

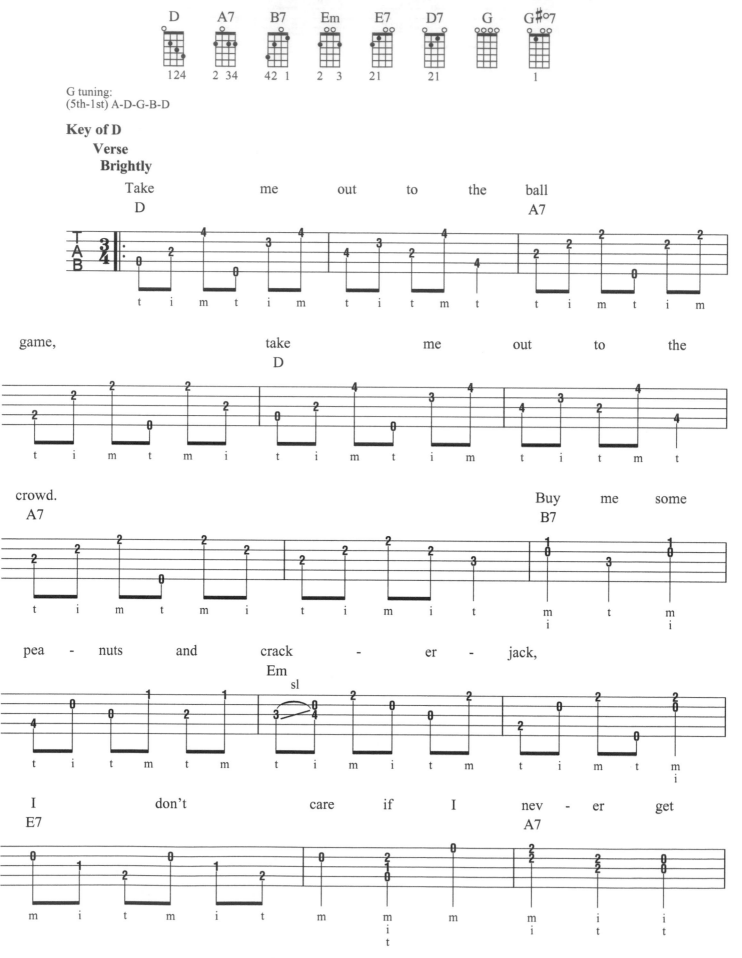

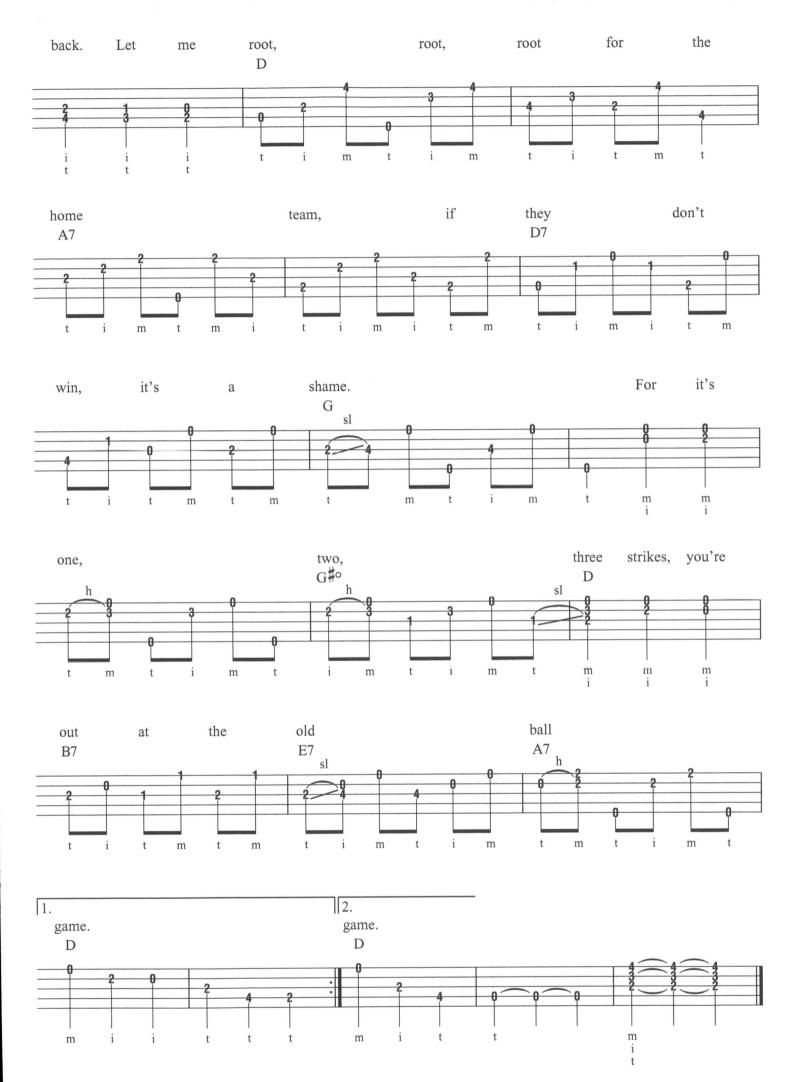

# That's All

## Words and Music by Bob Haymes and Alan E. Brandt

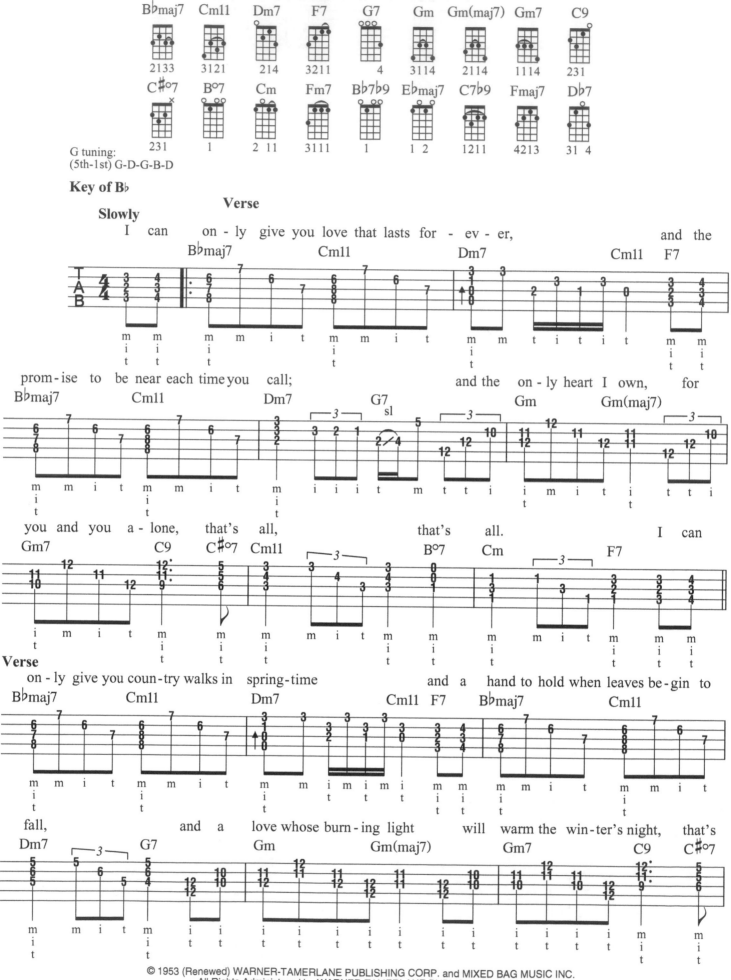

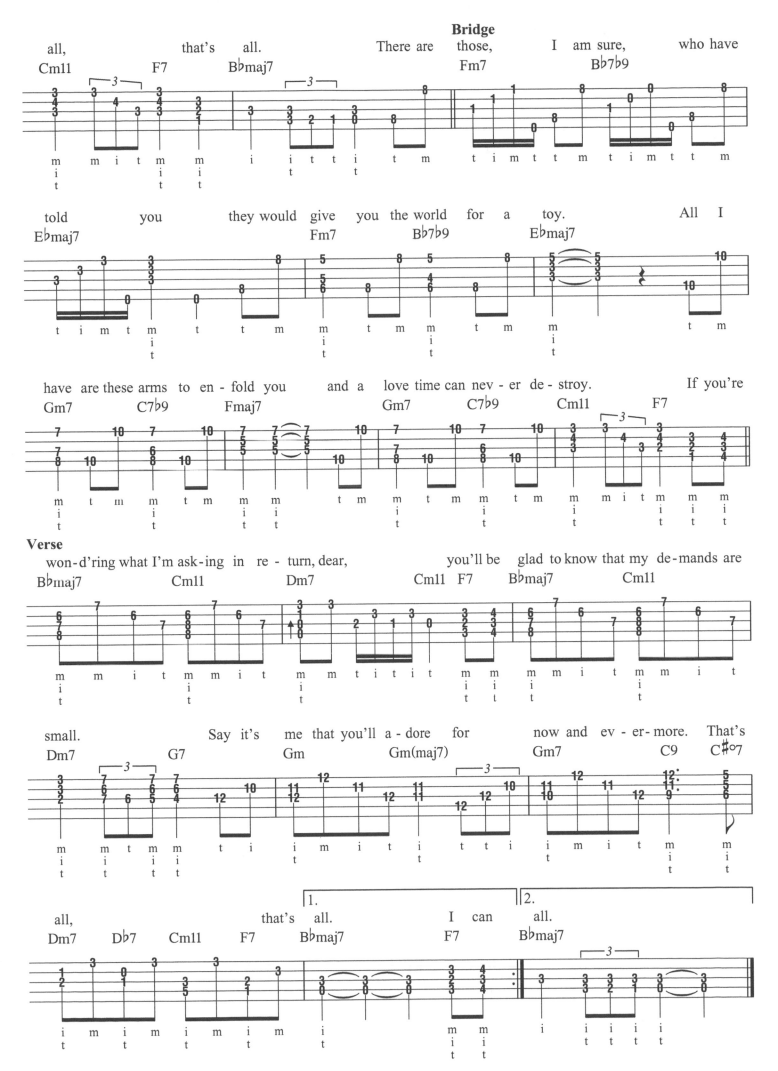

# There Will Never Be Another You

from the Motion Picture ICELAND

**Lyric by Mack Gordon**
**Music by Harry Warren**

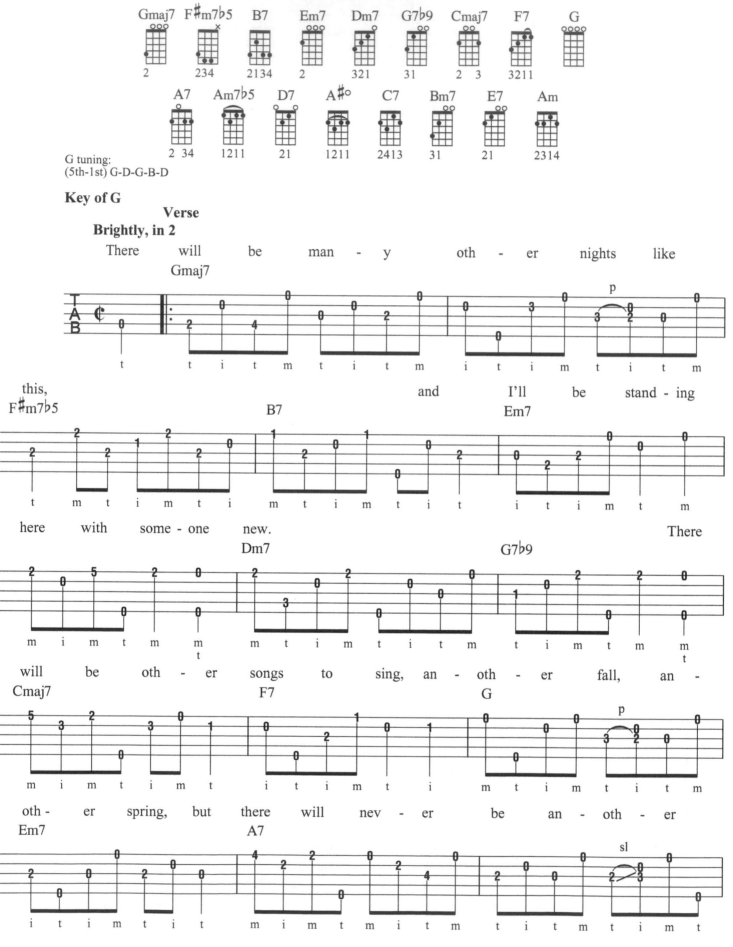

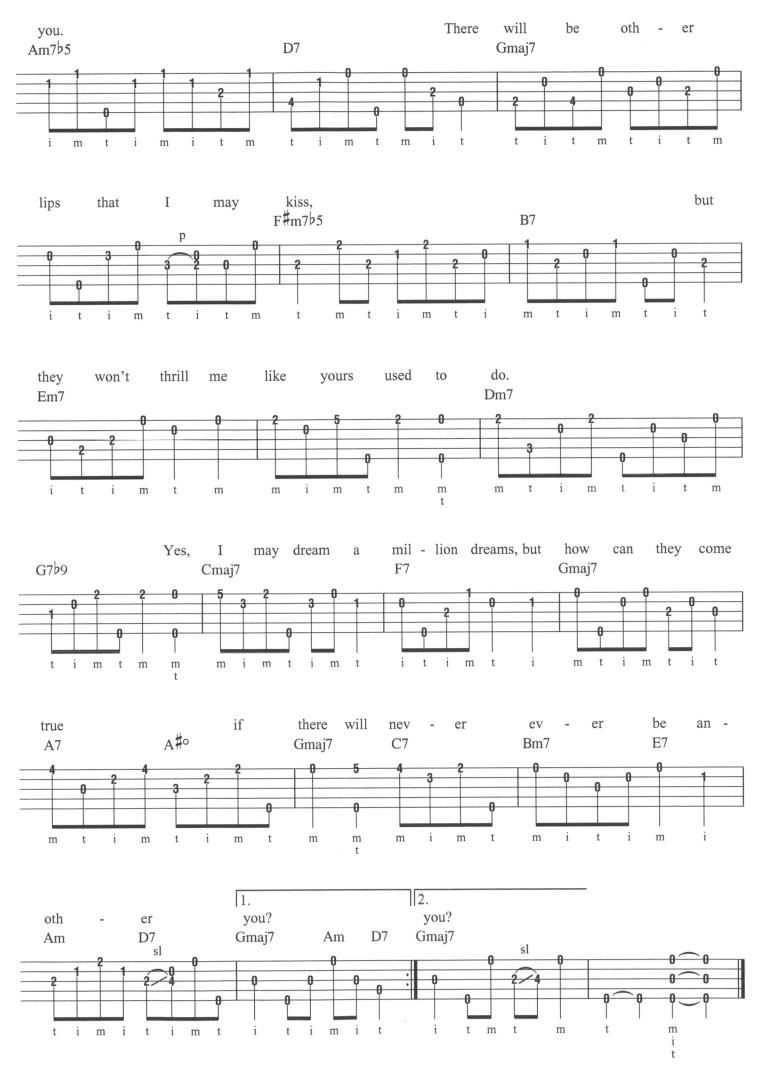

# Wait 'til the Sun Shines, Nellie

**Words by Andrew B. Sterling**
**Music by Harry von Tilzer**

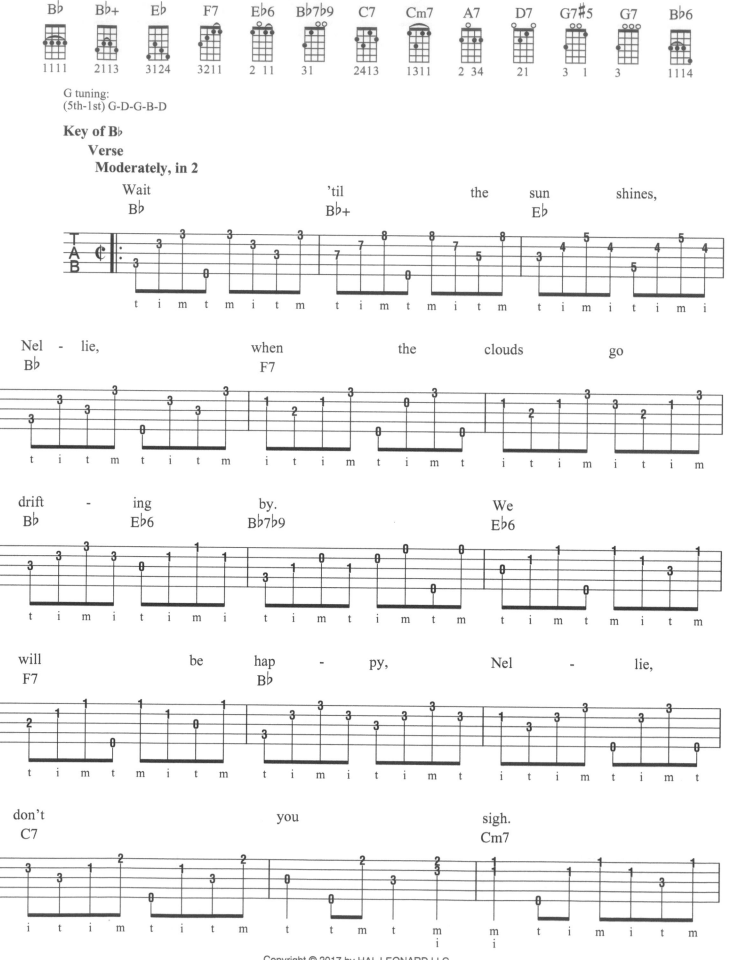

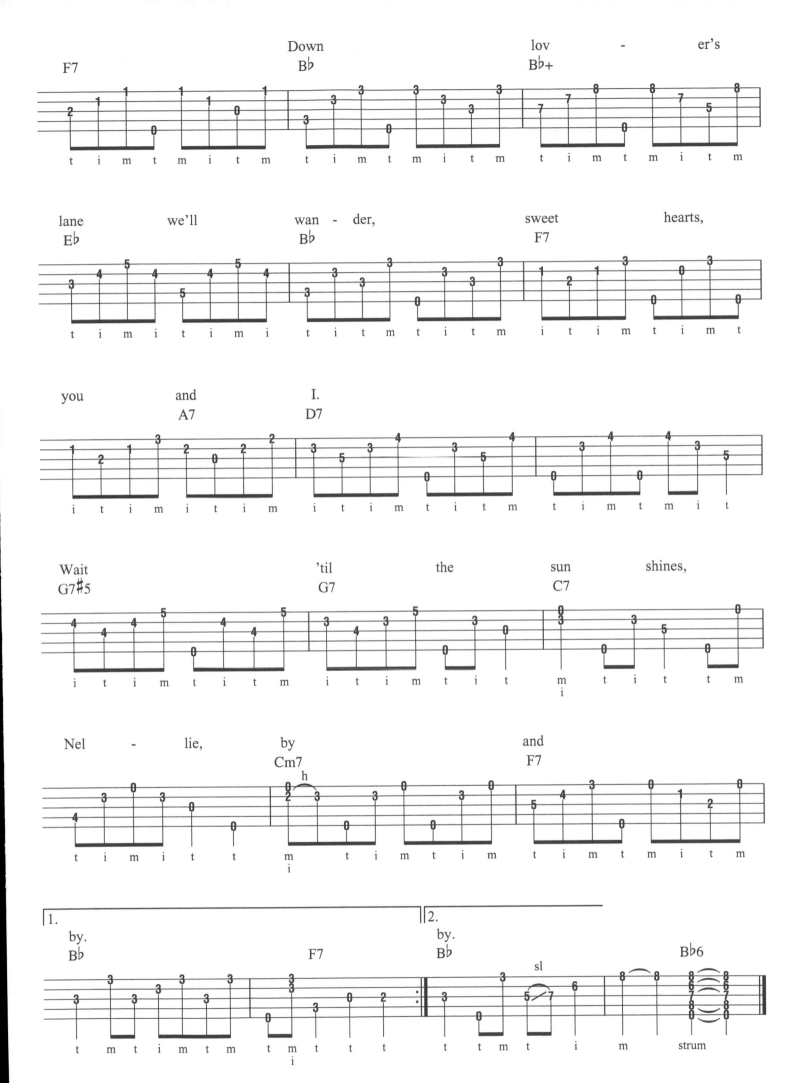

# The World Is Waiting for the Sunrise

**Words by Eugene Lockhart**
**Music by Ernest Seitz**

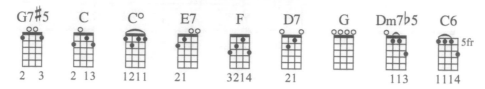

G tuning:
(5th-1st) G-D-G-B-D

**Key of C**

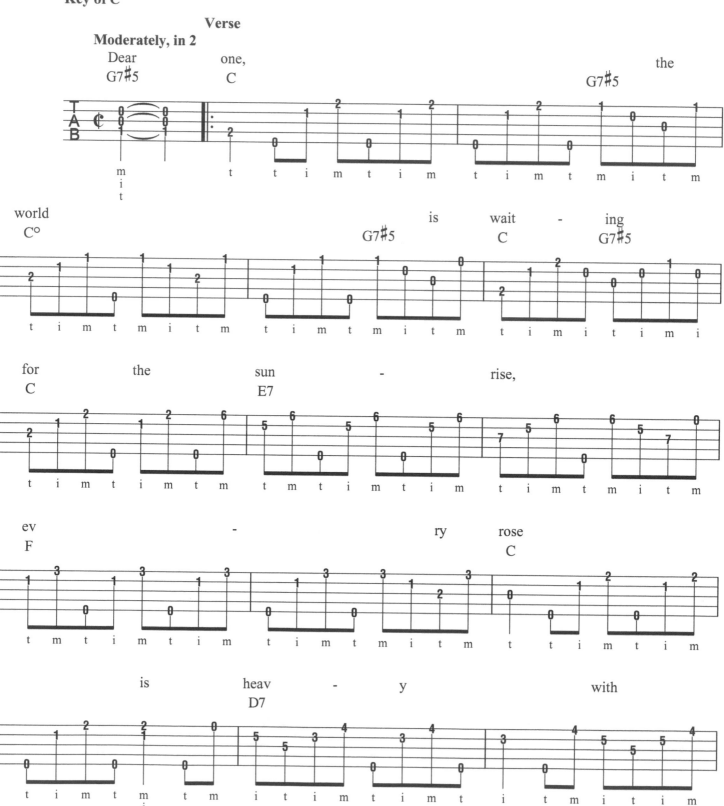

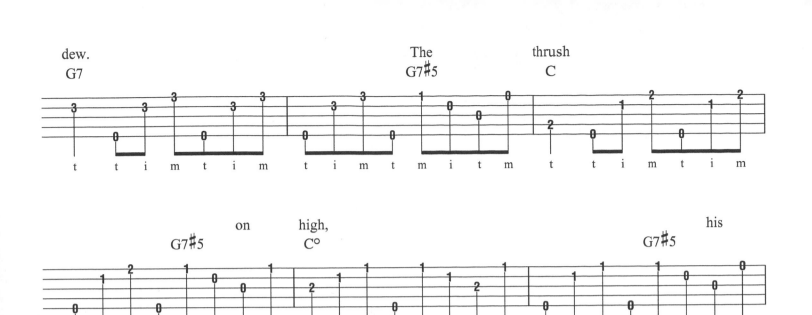

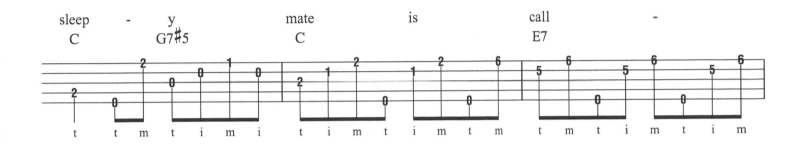

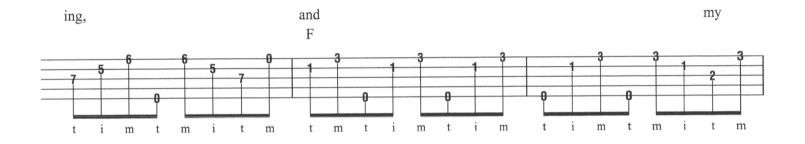

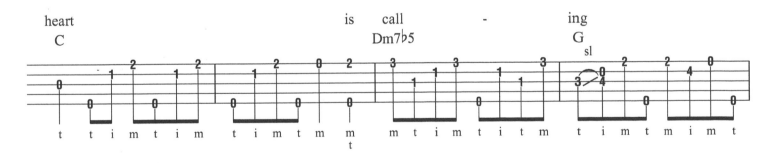

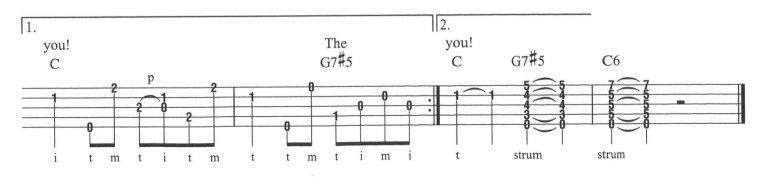

# BANJO NOTATION LEGEND

**TABLATURE** graphically represents the banjo fingerboard. Each horizontal line represents a string, and each number represents a fret.

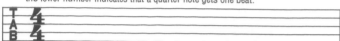

Strings:
1 D
2 B
3 G
4 D
5 G

4th string, 2nd fret      1st & 2nd strings open, played together

**TIME SIGNATURE:**
The upper number indicates the number of beats per measure, the lower number indicates that a quarter note gets one beat.

**CUT TIME:**
Each note's time value should be cut in half. As a result, the music will be played twice as fast as it is written.

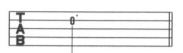

**QUARTER NOTE:**
time value = 1 beat

**EIGHTH NOTES:**
time value = 1/2 beat each

single    in series

**SIXTEENTH NOTES:**
time value = 1/4 beat each

single    in series

**DOTTED QUARTER NOTE:**
time value = 1 1/2 beat

**TIE:** Pick the 1st note only, then let it sustain for the combined time value.

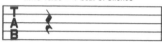

**TRIPLET:** Three notes played in the same time normally occupied by two notes of the same time value.

    ⌐— 3 —⌐

**GRACE NOTE:** A quickly played note with no time value of its own. The grace note and the note following it only occupy the time value of the second note.

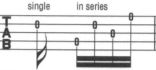

**RITARD:** A gradual slowing of the tempo or speed of the song.

*rit.*

**QUARTER REST:**
time value = 1 beat of silence

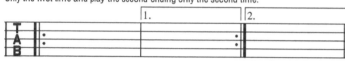

**EIGHTH REST:**
time value = 1/2 beat of silence

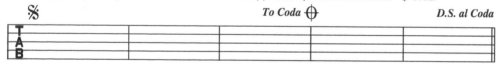

**HALF REST:**
time value = 2 beats of silence

**WHOLE REST:**
time value = 4 beats of silence

**ENDINGS:** When a repeated section has a first and second ending, play the first ending only the first time and play the second ending only the second time.

1.    2.

**REPEAT SIGNS:** Play the music between the repeat signs two times.

**D.S. AL CODA:**
Play through the music until you complete the measure labeled *"D.S. al Coda,"* then go back to the sign (𝄋).
Then play until you complete the measure labeled *"To Coda ⊕,"* then skip to the section labeled *"⊕ Coda."*

𝄋      *To Coda* ⊕      *D.S. al Coda*      ⊕ *Coda*

**HAMMER-ON:** Strike the first (lower) note with one finger, then sound the higher note (on the same string) with another finger by fretting it without picking.

h

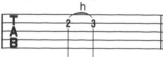

**PULL-OFF:** Place both fingers on the notes to be sounded. Strike the first note and without picking, pull the finger off to sound the second (lower) note.

p

**SLIDE UP:** Strike the first note and then slide the same fret-hand finger up to the second note. The second note is not struck.

s

**SLIDE DOWN:** Strike the first note and then slide the same fret-hand finger down to the second note. The second note is not struck.

s

**HALF-STEP CHOKE:** Strike the note and bend the string up 1/2 step.

1/2

**WHOLE-STEP CHOKE:** Strike the note and bend the string up one step.

1

**NATURAL HARMONIC:** Strike the note while the fret-hand lightly touches the string directly over the fret indicated.

Harm.

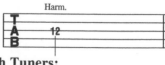

**BRUSH:** Play the notes of the chord indicated by quickly rolling them from bottom to top.

## Scruggs/Keith Tuners:

**HALF-TWIST UP:** Strike the note, twist tuner up 1/2 step, and continue playing.

1/2

**HALF-TWIST DOWN:** Strike the note, twist tuner down 1/2 step, and continue playing.

1/2

**WHOLE-TWIST UP:** Strike the note, twist tuner up one step, and continue playing.

1

**WHOLE-TWIST DOWN:** Strike the note, twist tuner down one step, and continue playing.

1

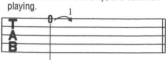

## Right Hand Fingerings

t = thumb    i = index finger    m = middle finger